Julia Morgan, Architect
and the Creation of the
Asilomar Conference Grounds

Julia Morgan, Architect
and the Creation of the
Asilomar Conference Grounds

INCLUDING A SPECIAL COMPARISON WITH
THE HEARST CASTLE

Russell L. Quacchia

Published by Q Publishing

Copyright © 2005 by Russell L. Quacchia.

Library of Congress Number: 2005901741
ISBN :   Hardcover   1-4134-8820-X
    Softcover   1-4134-8819-6

First Published 2005
Fourth Printing
This book was printed in the United States of America.

Library of Congress Cataloging in Publication Data

Russell L. Quacchia

Julia Morgan, Architect and the Creation of the Asilomar Conference Grounds

Includes Bibliographical References and Index

1. Architecture   2. Art History   3. Women's Studies

To order additional copies of this book, contact:
http://www.qpublishing-ca.com/

To
Sara Holmes Boutelle,
for her pioneering work in bringing Julia Morgan
to the attention of a larger audience.

Julia Morgan.

I did not know that talent was gender based!
—Julia Morgan

My buildings . . . will speak for me long after I'm gone.
—Julia Morgan

CONTENTS

i Preface 13

ii Acknowledgments 15

iii Introduction 19

1 Julia Morgan, Architect:
  A Biographical Sketch 23
2 The Ecole des Beaux-Arts:
  Architectural Training in Paris 58
3 The Arts and Crafts Movement: English Origins and the
  San Francisco Bay Region's Unique Version 72
4 The San Francisco Bay Region: Emerging Technologies
  and Institutions in the Formative Years 82
5 Julia Morgan's Two Largest Projects:
  Hearst Castle and Asilomar, a comparison 98
6 The Site of Asilomar, Pacific Grove:
  The Origins of a Monterey Bay Township 113
7 The Asilomar Conference Grounds: The Manner and
  Course of Its Founding 124
8 Asilomar's Julia Morgan Buildings:
  Artistically Considered 159
9 Asilomar's Julia Morgan Buildings:
  Experientially Considered 173

Concluding Remarks 188

Appendix A: Alta California: From Spanish Territory to the
    Gold Rush and Statehood 191
Appendix B: The Ecole des Beaux-Arts in Paris:
    Its History and Design Theory 206
Appendix C : Asilomar's Buildings and Improvements
    Designed by Julia Morgan 219
Appendix D: Julia Morgan: Chronology 221

Chapter Notes 223

Bibliography 235

Photography Credits 243

Index 245

About the Author 253

Map of California

PREFACE

Of the literally hundreds of building projects that the distinguished architect, Julia Morgan, designed over her long career, two of the largest, most complex and lengthy in years to complete were the "Hearst Castle" in San Simeon, California, for William Randolph Hearst and the Asilomar Conference Grounds in Pacific Grove, Monterey, California, for the Young Women's Christian Association (YWCA)[1]. These two commissions, awarded to the same architect to design, could not perhaps be in greater contrast in the nature of their origins, purpose, aesthetic character and social implications.

In terms of their public status, San Simeon's Hearst Castle is largely known. It is notable to tourism and has been much studied and documented by architectural historians and biographers of the Hearst family. It has been widely published in many forms from the scholarly to the touring interests. On the other hand, Asilomar, the focal project of this book, is comparatively unknown, unpublished, unstudied and undocumented. Yet both have been gifted to the California State Park System for preservation and use as significant monuments in California's architectural heritage. Hearst Castle was gifted in 1958 and Asilomar in 1956. These two facilities remain the most profitable of the entire state park system. The Hearst Castle is generally visited by tourists, more as an artifactual object of considerable visual interest, while Asilomar is intensely utilized as a retreat accommodation for scheduled conferences of many different kinds, including governmental, institutional and business meetings.

Julia Morgan worked on the Asilomar complex of buildings from 1912 until 1928. She worked on the Hearst Castle project from 1919 until 1942.

The very fact that these two major works of architecture have been honored by being held and cared for under the auspices of the state park system and additionally were placed on the Federal Registry of National Land Marks—and both were designed by the same architect, Julia Morgan—is to speak to the talent that authored their forms. These two very different projects coming from one single design personality has baffled some and amused others. But Julia Morgan practiced as an architect of the eclectic orientation striving to please her clients. Understood in this way her work on these two very different commissions is neither baffling nor amusing, although certainly intriguing, and testimony to a unique woman and architectural talent practicing in a very difficult milieu.

ACKNOWLEDGMENTS

I became interested in Julia Morgan and her work while undertaking training in architecture at the University of California, Berkeley. This interest was especially rekindled with several visits to Asilomar beginning in the late 1960s attending conferences. In this connection, a debt of gratitude, long overdue, is expressed to Professor William Hayes for his invitation as program chair and conference coordinator to participate, along with Professor Sara Holmes Boutelle, in presenting papers and discussion on Julia Morgan and her architecture to the American Society for Aesthetics, 1977 Pacific Division Conference held at Asilomar.

Many persons and institutions also play a role in the generation of a book such as this deserving acknowledgment.

My very personal thanks to Ms. Elizabeth McClave, a longtime tenant of Julia Morgan's apartment complex at 2229 Divisidero Street in San Francisco, California, for graciously inviting me to visit with her at her residence in Carmel Valley and providing some firsthand impressions of Julia Morgan.

I would extend my special thanks to Ranger Roxann Jacobus who oversees the Asilomar State Beach and Conference Grounds on behalf of the California State Parks, for sharing with me her caring interest and formidable knowledge of Asilomar's history.

In writing such a book as this, one heavily relies on the work of so many other authors who have gone before. The bibliography represents a list of some of those many who were consulted and are duly acknowledged with great appreciation. My sincere appreciation is also extended to the following: the archivists of the Department of Special Collections and University Archives of Leland Stanford University for their support in making available its extensive Pacific Improvement Company document files in doing primary source research for this book; the University of California College of Environmental Design Archives and Bancroft Libraries, Berkeley, for the help and courtesy extended to me in support of locating materials pertinent to understanding Julia Morgan's career; the Special Collection Department of the Robert F. Kennedy Library, at California Polytechnic State University and the Local History Department of the Harrison Memorial Library, Carmel-by-the-Sea, California, for making available valuable resource materials. It might be of interest to note the Harrison Library building was designed by Julia Morgan's friend and mentor, Bernard Maybeck, in 1926.

Also deserving of acknowledgment for assistance in locating and providing information and especially photographic materials are: The Special Collections Department of the F.W. Olin Library, Mills College; the Hearst Castle California State Parks, Archives and Photography Department; and the North Baker Research Library of the California Historical Society. My special thanks to Pat Hathaway, of California Views in Monterey, for making available, images from his considerable photographic collection in support of this book.

Special appreciation is accorded to Sharon Crawford and Carol Sheehan for reading early drafts and providing substantial guidance to making this a better and more readable book. To Kay Alexander for editorial expertise. Also to Allison Campbell, Taylor Coffman and Peter Kivy for each in their own way en-spiriting this project. Finally, perennial gratitude goes to my wife, Moira, for her patience and encouragement throughout.

INTRODUCTION

This book historically examines one of California's most distinguished architects, Julia Morgan, and one of this architect's largest and special projects, the Asilomar Conference Grounds in Pacific Grove, Monterey, California.

The underlying themes, which motivated me into writing the book, can be conveyed in four questions: How did Julia Morgan come to be born in San Francisco? How did she in a "groundbreaking" precedent way as a woman, become an architect? How did the Asilomar Conference Grounds, as one of her two major commissions, come to be founded? And why did Julia Morgan, as its sole architect, give to Asilomar's site planning and buildings the character and features they have? The answers are stories. Taken together they are, contextually, a California story that converges on the unique natural setting and cultural history of the greater San Francisco Bay Region. The wishful aim of the book is not just to provide a descriptive account but, hopefully, to induce some level of insight into the personality and one architectural masterwork created by that personality, Julia Morgan.

Developing Julia Morgan's personal story is perilously hampered by the virtual absence of autobiographical materials and information. Relatively little is directly known about her life and professional career. Much of what is known is anecdotal. This is so for two basic reasons, both due to Julia Morgan herself. First, Julia Morgan was in many ways rigorously private about her person and especially about her family. She was otherwise fully engaged and socially active in all other respects connected with being fully dedicated to her chosen profession. Secondly, and likely due to this disposition, she sought to discard many of her business documents, books and architectural drawings upon closing her office at retirement, which came about due to age and impaired health.[1] Also, relatively little is known to exist that materially records the founding and development of Asilomar. The major source in this respect was the available archives of the Pacific Improvement Company from which the YWCA was able to obtain the Pacific Grove property from the company's land holdings in Monterey County.[2]

Consequently, in order to impart a fuller impression of Julia Morgan, her life and architectural temperament, and the history and architecture of Asilomar, the story is served by providing a larger amount of contextual and circumstantial information than would otherwise usually be the case with such a successful figure. The strategy of the book is to provide several relatively independent "sketches," arrayed in chapters, beginning with a biography of Julia Morgan—her family, birth, upbringing and career. This is followed by three chapters about key factors that shaped Julia Morgan's architectural temperament—her training at the Ecole des Beaux-Arts in Paris, the very influential Arts and Crafts Movement, the advent of the San Francisco Bay Region's technologies and institutions that directly conditioned architectural practices and products at the time. The next chapter introduces and contrasts certain aspects of Julia Morgan's two largest and most complex projects: the Hearst Castle and Asilomar. This chapter serves as a transition for the following chapters where the focus turns to Monterey Peninsula's Pacific Grove, which is the township site of Asilomar, and the founding of Asilomar, respectively. In the final two chapters, the artistic qualities and experiences of

Julia Morgan's existing remaining buildings at Asilomar are considered.

The Julia Morgan and Asilomar stories taken together as indicated are a California story. For those who may not be familiar with California's history, appendix A provides a brief history of California as the background from which the very inauguration, thrust, energy and mood of our story takes shape. For those who may have special interests in architectural education or architectural theory, appendix B provides a brief history of the very influential Ecole des Beaux-Arts from its inception to its closure in 1960 and the development of its architectural design teachings to which Julia Morgan was exposed as a student. Appendix C gives a listing of all the buildings and improvements that Julia Morgan designed for Asilomar, and appendix D provides a convenient referential chronology of Julia Morgan.

The chapters and appendices are designed in a format that constitutes a continuous narrative story yet, hopefully, allows the reader, with varying or special interests—be they biography, women's studies, local history, architectural history, education, theory of design, or simply visiting Asilomar (or by contrast visiting Hearst Castle at San Simeon)—to approach the book's chapters in selectively different ways to satisfy particular inclinations. The book at moments takes the reader into areas fairly esoteric to the architectural way of life or to the advent of Asilomar itself. While needful, hopefully these forays will prove more interesting than strenuous.

The social character of the times during which Julia Morgan lived and practiced her art was not friendly to professional women, especially one pursuing an architectural profession. Julia Morgan, in this regard on one occasion, retorted to a soliloquy by a questioning antagonist that she "did not know that talent was gender based." [3] Julia Morgan's talent is attested to by the continuing vitality of the architectural environment of Asilomar that we find today, and affirms her comment that "my buildings will be my legacy . . . they will speak for me long after I'm gone." Given Julia Morgan's proneness to professional anonymity, I suspect that if she were asked today to herself supply some autobiographical details for a book such as this, she would respond in the following way: "Just say that Julia Morgan is an architect of whom nothing is known. Now let us have a look at her buildings."

JULIA MORGAN, ARCHITECT:
A BIOGRAPHICAL SKETCH

The architect of the Asilomar Conference Grounds, Julia Morgan, was an extraordinary woman and an exceptional architect with a long and prolific professional career. She is considered to be the first woman-architect of prominence in the nation. She is certainly the most significant woman-architect in the history of California. No figure has emerged to challenge this honor.[1]

Julia Morgan's significance lies in two impressive themes. First is her personality, temperament and achievements, as a woman, pursuing a formal education in architecture and undertaking to establish an independent practice in a field entirely dominated by men and habitually assumed and accepted to be so by society in general; second, as a professional architect, is her remarkable talent and abilities for producing such a large number of varying kinds and sizes of buildings, all with an exceptionally sophisticated excellence.

Julia Morgan was born in San Francisco on January 20, 1872, to Charles and Eliza Morgan. She was the second of five children: her elder brother Parmelee, her younger sister Emma, and two younger brothers Avery and Gardiner (Sam). The latter three children were born in Oakland, a suburban community located on the eastern edge of San Francisco Bay where the family had permanently moved in 1873.[2] In that year the Morgan's purchased property on Fourteenth and Brush streets, in a fashionable neighborhood, and they're built a large three-story Victorian-style home. This was to be the house that Julia would grow up in and, after her higher education years in Berkeley and Paris, was to come back to and live with her family until the mid-1920s. In that decade Julia Morgan purchased two adjoining houses in San Francisco and converted them into a single building forming several rental apartments at 2229 Divisidero Street. Keeping one apartment for herself, this remained her home until her death in February 1957 at the age of eighty-five, just seven years after closing her architectural practice.

Julia Morgan was diminutive in stature and of a quiet manner belying a forcefully dynamic and energetic personality. She stood just about five feet tall and weighed little over one hundred pounds. She carried herself with an erect gait and was always immaculately dressed, even at construction sites, in a dark dress suit, with men's pants beneath, white silk blouse and "Queen Ann" style hat. She was endowed with a great deal of stamina, a strong will, a fearlessness and keen intelligence. These traits were joined with an artistic sense and a technical interest in how things were made and worked. During her architectural career she did not carry a purse and used her suit pockets well, always, famously, full of pens, pencils, scale and drawing pads. She was often described as being a "striking" or "handsome" woman. She was a socially friendly person, caring of her family, those she employed, rented to, or otherwise came into contact with, inclusive of her clients. She had a firmness when it came to proprieties and manners. Julia Morgan was known to be of enormous will and determination, firm in her pursuits and was said not to suffer fools lightly. She admired personal courage and was herself fearless, often climbing out through windows onto construction scaffolding and planks at heights of thirteen stories in order to inspect workmanship.

She once hired a pilot who owned a two-seater airplane just to experience what it was like to fly and, later, before it was commonplace, chartered a Lockheed-Vega, a fully enclosed cabin aircraft, to fly to construction sites. Despite her reputation for privacy and anonymity, which contrasted how deeply known she was, Julia Morgan maintained several affiliations with formal groups. Among these were the YWCA, the Baptist Church located near her home in Oakland where she attended services, though she and her family were Presbyterians; the Kappa Alpha Theta, Omega Chapter sorority house at the University of California, Berkeley, which she joined while a student; the San Francisco Women's Athletic Club; and the prestigious Century Club of California.[3] Julia Morgan became a member of the American Institute of Architects in 1921, her only professional affiliation.

Julia Morgan's stamina for work was extraordinary. She sustained great energy and ate sporadically and little. She thought nothing of working eighteen-hour days, drinking black coffee and consuming candy bars. She often left her lodgings for her office before dawn and returned after one or two o'clock in the morning, when she was not traveling to distant projects. She hardly ever turned away a commission, no matter how small or how difficult, and always treated each with equal favor and fervor. She once metaphorically remarked in the latter connection: "It is very poor policy to say that one child is better than another child." She addressed her work as a perfectionist and with a practical, no-nonsense manner. In this respect she once remarked to one of her draftspersons who, apparently ignoring "the facts of life," had drawn up a stairway that could not be possibly built, "Well, young man," she said, "I can't deal with fiction writers."

Julia Morgan had a special fondness for her native state's landscape and was particularly attracted to the Monterey and Carmel areas. She often visited these places, when she was

younger, with her family on weekend trips by Southern Pacific
train. She eventually purchased and kept a small studio-
residence near Franklin Street, in Monterey, as a retreat
location.[4]

Julia Morgan was a woman striving for "accomplishment"
in a male-dominated territory against widespread social
prejudice in a profession she simply loved for what it could
accomplish. She distinguished between two different
concepts of publicity: one that was being sought by virtue
of self-promotion and glorification, and the other that was
gained by virtue of earned and notable reputation in the
sense of credit due. She favored and worked hard on behalf
of the latter.

An advocate of discipline, Eliza, Julia Morgan's mother,
was of high moral temperament. She actively nurtured her
children in morals, manners and education, encouraging
preparations for their choice of careers. She appears to have
instilled the notion, noted above, that one should strive to be
a person of "accomplishment."

Julia's father, Charles Morgan, was born and raised in
New Bedford, Connecticut. He was a mining engineer by
training and had sailed from Connecticut around South
America to California in 1867. He had aspirations of
becoming a sugar commodities broker in Hawaii, but during
his stay in San Francisco he became enamored with both
the beauty of its setting and the prospects for making his own
fortune speculating in minerals and other ventures. He
returned to his home in the East and married Eliza Parmelee
in 1869. Almost immediately the couple came West on the
newly completed transcontinental railroad and took
residency in a family hotel on Van Ness Avenue in San
Francisco where they were residing at the time of Julia
Morgan's birth.

Charles Morgan, an easygoing person, tested his luck and fortune in a string of ventures, investing in stores, mines and other businesses, but to no great profit and sometimes, considerable loss. At one point in July 1878, such financial issues compelled Eliza Morgan and her children to return to her family in New York where they stayed, returning to Oakland a year later in June 1879. It was during this visit that Julia Morgan became ill with scarlet fever and also suffered an inflammatory mastoid infection behind an ear. The latter ailment would return to cause her serious problems in advanced age. Charles Morgan later became part owner in the Shasta Iron Works, a manufacturing company, ran for public office, served on various state commissions and served as the director of Oakland's public school system. He always maintained an office in San Francisco and Julia Morgan frequently accompanied him on the bay crossing trips by boat from Oakland's port to San Francisco's ferry building.

The Morgan family lived in early financial comfort due in good part to the generosity of Eliza's father, Albert Parmelee, whose own considerable fortune was made from brokering cotton futures on the New York Commodity Exchange prior to the Civil War. San Francisco had been a fast-growing, "rough-and-tumble" metropolis since 1848, the year in which California became a U.S. territory, and when gold was discovered at John Sutter's sawmill, the frenzy of migration to the area ensued. When Charles Morgan arrived in 1870, mining corporations remained active and some still expanding. Despite that the peak of the gold rush was beginning to wane, new silver and gold lodes were being discovered. These decades saw major events in America, such as the completion of the transcontinental railroad in 1869, which induced migration and stimulated communications throughout the country. It was also a period manifesting considerable scientific advancements and along with the creation of new technologies such as electricity, telephone, automobile and typewriter, among many others. The nation was enjoying economic prosperity and high employment, contributing to improved general living conditions and, significantly, generating a large middle class along with a moderate size upper middle class.

Julia Morgan attended Oakland grammar and high schools. At that time these public schools were serving, for the most part, the children of prominent and well-to-do families. They had the ambiance of private schools. Julia Morgan was an earnest student, excelling in mathematics, sciences and music, earning a scholarly reputation. She learned to play the piano, but her success with the violin was such that she would later be invited to perform solo at certain gatherings while attending the university in Berkeley. At this early stage she also manifested a keen interest in the sciences and the mechanics of things, that is to say, how things worked and how they were put together. In her last year at Oakland High School, which she entered in 1886 at the age of fourteen, Julia Morgan indicated to her parents her desire to have a career of some kind, perhaps in music or medicine, and wished to continue her education at the nearby University of California in Berkeley that had opened in 1868. This wish certainly ran against the grain of fashion of the day for young women. But Julia Morgan's parents, prizing education, fully supported the notion as they did with all their children.

Julia Morgan entered the university in 1890, traveling there from her Oakland home each day by horse-drawn streetcar with her brother Avery as escort. Eventually she was routinely accompanied by her sister Emma, who herself was studying law, or her school friend Jessica Peixotto, who was pursuing economics. Julia Morgan's undergraduate work was in mathematics and the physical sciences. These subjects were very unusual for women to study and she often was the only woman in class. Gender bias was an issue Julia Morgan would have to endure and challenge in her own unique way throughout her life. With so few women in the university at the beginning of her freshman year, Julia Morgan joined the newly established Kappa Alpha Theta sorority. Located in a rented house adjacent to the campus, it was the first sorority to open at the university, with twenty-seven originating pledges. One of them was Julia's sister, Emma. It is in this connection as a sorority member that Julia Morgan may have first met the philanthropist Phoebe Apperson Hearst, who was an active patron of the sorority and who had a residence immediately nearby where she hosted tea parties and other gatherings for the sorority. Julia Morgan, some fifteen years later in 1908, would become the architect for the sorority's new house at 2723 Durant Street in Berkeley. She would also, just two years earlier, design a residence for her grade school friend, sorority sister and later traveling companion to Paris, Jessica Peixotto, located at 2225 College Avenue in Berkeley in 1906.

During her university undergraduate work at Berkeley, Julia Morgan arrived at her decision to be an architect. This commitment was influenced by Julia Morgan's youthful trips East to visit family relations. Charles and Eliza Morgan traveled East to join with their parents for the purpose of having each of the newborn children be christened in the family's favored Grace Church in Brooklyn Heights. Eliza Morgan often went on her own to visit as well, taking along all her children. There Julia Morgan could visit her mother's cousin, Lucy Thornton, who was married to Pierre LeBrun, an architect and member of Napoleon LeBrun & Sons, a prestigious New York firm that had designed the New York Metropolitan Life Insurance building, among other significant monumental works. Julia Morgan had always been impressed by the work he was involved with, and LeBrun in turn always recognized and encouraged her interest and advocated that she enroll in the College of Engineering at Berkeley. At that time there was no architecture program at the university. Julia Morgan's training in the Engineering College was in technical subjects, learning about the structural aspects of buildings and gaining expertise in how to calculate with mathematical formulas the strength and required sizes of structural components of buildings such as load-bearing walls, columns, trusses and beams. At the time, Professor Frank Soule was the head of the college. A specialist in structural design, especially wood trusses, he had come to the university from the Army Corps of Engineers. During one of her civil engineering courses, she developed a paper on structural stress analysis entitled "A Structural Analysis of the Steel Frame of the Mills Building in San Francisco," which was later awarded a review comment by the San Francisco architect, A. Page Brown, that only two or three practicing professional engineers were capable of understanding it. She also learned how to do technical construction drawings and became familiar with the economics of construction techniques. Bernard Maybeck, who was to become her good friend and mentor, arrived to teach descriptive geometry and drawing techniques in 1894. Realizing that most of his students were inclined to architecture rather than engineering, he decided to hold informal meetings on the subject at his home, which Julia Morgan was known to have attended.

In 1894 Julia Morgan graduated from the University of California with a Bachelor of Science degree in civil engineering, the third woman to have ever done so. For a short time immediately after graduation, Julia Morgan worked and studied with Bernard Maybeck, who encouraged her to go to the Ecole des Beaux-Arts in Paris to complete her education in architecture. He was in the position to fully appreciate that she needed to complement her technical training with knowledge of subjects she lacked, such subjects essential to architecture as architectural history and particularly design theory in the areas of functional organization and aesthetic manipulation of space, the latter involving massing, proportion, composition and decoration. Julia Morgan discussed her desire to become an architect with her parents, and seeing her confidence and determination, they gave their consent for her to undertake a trip eastward by train with her friend, Jessica Peixotto, to visit Morgan's relatives, including the LeBruns. The plan was to visit and evaluate existing architecture schools in the East Coast and from there travel on to France, even though entering the Ecole des Beaux-Arts appeared to be at the time a very remote possibility.

In March 1896, at the age of twenty-four, Julia Morgan left by boat from New York for Paris with Jessica Peixotto who, herself also having graduated from the University of California at Berkeley, was to study graduate-level economics there. Accommodations had been prearranged for them at the Club for American Women on the Rue de Chevreuse located in Paris's left bank. While preparing herself for the possibility of entering the Ecole, which even to date had not allowed women to enroll, she joined the atelier of Marcel de Monclos, whom Bernard Maybeck knew while he was at the Ecole. Students regularly studied in ateliers with independent practicing architects who provided instruction, oversight on design work, and needed guidance in entering school competitions. Julia Morgan later joined the atelier of Benjamin Chasussemiche when De Monclos's studio closed. The Ecole decided in 1897, apparently influenced in part by Bernard Maybeck, to allow women to take the entrance exams for the very first time. Julia Morgan wrote to her cousins Lucy and Pierre LeBrun in July 1897 reporting that it had been "suddenly" announced that the Ecole des Beaux-Arts examination would be open to women for the first time. Given only a few weeks of notice and rather than delaying to take the exams she prepared quickly. She did so under the guise of a long-standing student maxim, which advises that it is necessary to fail at least one time to learn how to take the exams. While she had passed all of them, she failed to rank high enough for admission.[5]

Julia Morgan did not permit herself to become dejected over the experience even upon learning that "the mark" she received from the jury was motivated by the wish "not to encourage young girls." The experience only strengthened her resolve even more.[6] In her third attempt at taking the exams, Julia Morgan was successful, placing thirteenth out of over three hundred applicants in October 1898. She became the first woman to enter the Ecole, a 250-year-old institution. While in her second year of attendance, Maybeck and Phoebe Hearst arrived in Paris to represent the international competition for the University of California campus plan and building program. During their stay, they both took considerable interest in Julia's welfare and her schoolwork. In 1901, at the maximum age limit of thirty, a constraint set by Ecole policy, Julia Morgan entered her last possible student architectural competition that required her to design a monumental palace theater. She won in the competition and was awarded the first prize for which she had accrued enough credit points to earn her "diploma" certificate, the first one that was ever granted to a woman. After graduation from the Ecole, Julia Morgan stayed on in Paris to work for Benjamin Chasussemiche designing the Harriet Fearing residence located in Fontainebleau.

Julia Morgan returned to Oakland, California, in 1902 looking for employment. She visited Bernard Maybeck, who had little work in his office at the time but guided her to the office of John Galen Howard, himself a graduate of the Ecole des Beaux-Arts and the head of the newly formed Architectural School at the University of California, Berkeley. Howard was also the university's supervising architect for overall campus planning development. Julia Morgan joined the firm to work on the new Hearst Mining Building to be constructed at the university, which Phoebe Hearst was funding as a memorial to her husband, George Hearst, a mining magnate and U.S. senator. Upon its completion, Mrs. Hearst was so pleased with the outcome of this building that she requested Julia Morgan be the lead designer for another of the Hearst's planned gifts to the university, the new outdoor semicircular amphitheater for the campus based on the early Greek models of antiquity. This project was technically unique in that Julia Morgan proposed the construction be entirely of steel-reinforced concrete material.

Julia Morgan had been anxious to start up her own office and when it became known to her that John Galen Howard was said to have boasted that he had a wonderful woman-designer, "to whom I have to pay almost nothing," she moved to do so quickly. In 1904, she took the state examination for certification as an architect. She passed and became the first woman to be licensed as an architect in California. Along with working for John Galen Howard, she had also been designing for her own clients at the carriage house of the family home in Oakland, which she had converted into a drafting studio.

In 1904 she decided to open a small office at 456 Montgomery Street in San Francisco. John Galen Howard did not forgive Julia for leaving his office and used his influence as supervising architect for the university's building program to prevent Julia Morgan from securing commissions for campus buildings for many years. Even in 1915, at the time of the Panama-Pacific International Exposition in San Francisco, the committee of architect qualification and selection headed by Howard did not include Julia Morgan— even though she was already well known and established— among the architects to be considered to design buildings. It was only after considerable lobbying for a women's building to be included in the exposition that, at the behest of Mrs.

Phoebe Hearst, Julia Morgan was appointed to design the interior only of their building. In 1906, two years after opening her Montgomery Street office, the great San Francisco earthquake struck. While the building survived the earthquake, her office was destroyed that night by fire. Lost were all of her drafting tools, materials and records as well as a portion of her valuable reference library. The other portion of her library collection was stored at the family home in Oakland to which she was forced to temporarily return and work on commissions. Julia Morgan had developed a considerable collection of folios and architectural books while at the Ecole in Paris. During her office practice, these were used as a major reference tool for developing design conceptions in conferences with clients. In latter years, when her cousin, Pierre LeBrun, closed his office upon retiring, he shipped his architectural library collection to her. Many of these books were quite large in size, leather bound and heavy but always actively consulted for establishing the design direction a project might take.

At the time of the great earthquake, Julia Morgan had completed two projects, the Bell-Clock Campanile and the Margaret Carnegie Library building, at Mills College in Oakland, under her own independent practice. These two structures and the Hearst Mining and Greek Theater projects noted earlier, for which she was the designer in John Galen Howard's office, all survived the great earthquake without any damage. She then began to receive a number of commissions such that by the summer of 1907 she moved her office into a suite on the thirteenth floor of the Merchants Exchange Building at 465 California Street. This building was constructed in 1903, designed by the Chicago architect Daniel H. Burnham, and survived the earthquake quite well. Julia was to practice from this office for the remainder of her forty-seven-year career. Ira Wilson Hoover left John Galen Howard's office where he was chief draftsman to join Julia

Morgan as a junior partner in 1904. He left the office to return to the East Coast in 1910 to develop his own practice there. This was the only known partnership she ever formed, although there is some indication that Thaddeus Joy, an architectural draftsman, may have had a special position in the office and his name on the office door for a time.

A few months after the earthquake the owners of the burned-out Fairmont Hotel on Nob Hill in San Francisco had contacted the famous New York architect Stanford White, a partner in the firm of McKim, Mead & White, to restore the badly damaged building. In a poignant turn of events, Stanford White always "the ladies' man", was shot to death by Harry K. Thaw, a jealous husband of one of his many paramours, Evelyn Nesbit, just prior to getting the job under way. The Fairmont's owners turned to Julia Morgan to do the job largely based on her reputation as being very knowledgeable about reinforced concrete material and construction techniques. She was hired because of her abilities despite having opened her office only recently and being a woman. This reputation for competency was to serve her well in overcoming many business and social prejudices.

Facing the challenge of structurally reconstructing the Fairmont Hotel was not the only one Julia Morgan encountered with this commission. In typical fashion of the day, it was assumed that the only connection a woman could have with architecture was as an interior decorator. One day, Jane Armstrong, a reporter from the San Francisco Call newspaper who was visiting the job site covering the project's progress, turned to Julia Morgan and commented, "How you must have reveled in this chance to squeeze dry the loveliest tubes in the whole world of color." Julia Morgan responded, "I don't think you understand just what my work here has been. The decorative part was all done by a New York firm. In fact, most of it was finished before the fire and has been restored . . . my work here has been all structural." [7]This is thought to be the one and only "interview" ever held with Julia Morgan. The Fairmont Hotel reconstruction project brought much recognition to Julia Morgan and proved to be a major impetus to her career.

Julia Morgan was to complete over seven hundred projects in the course of her architectural practice. These projects ranged over many different building types, including houses, churches, schools, libraries, hospitals, clubs, gymnasia, apartments and YWCA chapter buildings. Her success in gaining commissions was due to a combination of circumstantial and personal factors. Julia Morgan was virtually the only native-born architect in the area. Unlike others, she was able to draw on many friends and family contacts. Her practice coincided with the expansion of the middle and upper classes seeking housing in and around the Bay Area. She had two special patrons who were significant to her practice, the philanthropist Pheobe Apperson Hearst and her son William Randolph Hearst, both sources of many commissions. Also at the time various women's organizations were being established and growing in influence and respect. Many of these, and in particular the YWCA, were to engage Julia Morgan as their architect. In the larger circumstances there were the nationwide events mentioned earlier; the volume of industrial production in the nation had doubled in the first twenty-five years of Julia Morgan's life, and a diversity of new inventions had appeared. But a large share of her success must be attributed to her own determination and ability to win people's confidence, respect and admiration through dedication and competency in all aspects of her chosen field. Unlike other architects, Julia Morgan relied solely on her reputation for talent and competency to procure work. While she maintained membership in certain organizations, she did not actively promote herself; she, for the most part, avoided social gatherings and shunned publicity. She did not speak or write on architecture. She did not actively serve in any professional associations; she would not be interviewed and even refused to post her name at building sites. The only breach to this overall posture was the occasion in which the architect-engineer Walter Steilberg, working in the office in 1913, wrote and released with innocent presumption, much to the chagrin and perhaps wrath of Julia Morgan, an article entitled "Some Examples of the Work of Julia Morgan", solicited by the professional periodical The Architect & Engineer of California. This would be the only known material to ever be provided by her office to any publication during her professional career.

Julia Morgan treated her financial status with great privacy and modesty. What income she earned, which was very moderate in the early phase of her career, was generously shared with employees or supporting someone in need. Eventually she achieved for herself the status of being "a women of means" for the most part by means of work on the Hearst Castle project for William Randolph Hearst.[8]

Julia Morgan was well known for being a client-oriented architect. Common to all architectural design approaches there usually is an underlying view about a way of life. Significant to Julia Morgan's design approach are her views on the architect's role in society and the relationship between life and architecture. Julia viewed the architect as a servant anonymously contributing to the various practical and aesthetic needs and wants of people. The architect, in her conception, is not that of a "master" with an "artistic ego" introducing novelty and drama into people's lives, reducing them to a spectator audience. Rather the architect is seen as an unobtrusive crafter of building designs to serve as a circumambient backdrop and whose form and characteristics are conditioned by the variable activities to be accommodated. For Julia Morgan the architect's role is to serve one's client, and architecture is preeminently a pragmatic undertaking to support and enhance the client's way of life. This is not to say that the architect's relationship to client or patron was entirely self-effacing. Julia Morgan would certainly produce the result she also wanted. While clients always had the opportunity to spell out their needs and express aesthetic preferences according to their tastes, Julia Morgan would then bring all her talent and abilities to bear upon this information under the guiding precept of "propriety." The one theoretical proposition Julia was apparently fond of quoting was the nineteenth-century theorist A. W. N. Pugin's view that architectural design consists in "commodity, firmness and propriety." The word "propriety" is to be taken here in the sense of observing decorum, aptness, fittingness or rightness, in both a moral and non-moral sense. Julia Morgan was not given to theorizing. She was an "imagist" and preferred to speak with architecture rather than about it. Whatever academic principles guided her design sensibilities, one has to find them embodied in her buildings.

In her approach to design, Julia Morgan drew mainly upon four principal sources of experience for her design precepts. Two of these derived from her formal training in academic institutions: her initial training in engineering and construction at the University of California at Berkeley, her exposure to "academic eclecticism" at the Ecole in Paris, supplemented by her travels in Europe. The two others derived from her birthplace: the San Francisco Bay Area's unique form of the "Arts and Crafts Movement" and the unique technological and institutional developments of the Bay Region's construction history along with the special qualities of California's natural environmental setting. All of these influences are exemplified variously in her architecture, but all four are uniquely present in her site planning and buildings that make up the Asilomar Conference Grounds. Of these four significant influences shaping Julia Morgan's architectural temperament, the Ecole des Beaux-Arts in Paris, the Arts and Crafts Movement, and the San Francisco Bay Region's construction technology and institutional history will be especially introduced.

Julia Morgan at age 7.

Kappa Alpha Theta Sorority Sisters, 1894
(Julia Morgan standing top left).

Morgan Family Residence, 14th and Brush Streets, Oakland.

Julia Morgan's Residence, 2229 Divisidero St., San Francisco

Bernard Maybeck, circa 1889

John Galen Howard, circa 1910.

Phoebe Apperson Hearst, circa 1893.

William Randolph Hearst, circa 1935.

Hearst Memorial Mining Building, U. C. Berkeley,
Dedicated 1907

Hearst Memorial Mining Building, U. C. Berkeley
(Entrance Foyer).

Hearst Greek Theater, U. C. Berkeley, Dedicated 1903.

The Campanile, Mills College, Oakland, Dedicated 1904.

The Margaret Carnegie Library, Mills College,
Oakland, Dedicated 1906.

The Margaret Carnegie Library, Mills College, Oakland
(Main Reading Room).

The Fairmont Hotel, Nob Hill, San Francisco, at the aftermath
of the Great Earthquake, 1906.

St. Johns Presbyterian Church, Berkeley 1910.

St. Johns Presbyterian Church, Berkeley
(View from entrance toward front altar).

St. Johns Presbyterian Church, Berkeley
(View from altar toward entrance).

THE ECOLE DES BEAUX-ARTS:
ARCHITECTURAL TRAINING IN PARIS

Upon earning her civil engineering degree from the University of California, the school Julia Morgan chose for her architectural training was the historically renowned and prestigious academy, the Ecole des Beaux-Arts in Paris. The development of this educational institution was a major force on architectural ideas and practices since the seventeenth century, especially so in the nineteenth century. By this time professional education in most Western countries followed the lead set in France. The beginning of this school provided a new basis, depth and soundness of training that eventually led to the formal recognition of the academically trained professional architect. It did so at the expense of the age-old forms of guildsman-master, and also the amateur, as building constructors. The Ecole over time emerged as the prototypical model for developing architectural schools throughout the Western world, including the United States. The early establishment in America of "Beaux-Arts-oriented architectural schools," such as MIT and Cornell, are examples. By the mid-nineteenth century it became the fashion for students of other countries, including the United States, to study in Paris. The first American to do so was the architect Richard Morris Hunt who attended in 1846 and was followed by many others.

Without any assured prospects of being admitted to the academy, Julia Morgan traveled to New York with Jessica

Peixotto as her companion. From there they both sailed to Paris, arriving in June 1896. After they had settled in their prearranged lodgings, Julia Morgan made contacts with friends of Bernard Maybeck, relying on his letters of introduction, and began to study French. She familiarized herself with the city and its architecture, all in pursuit of gaining admittance to an "atelier" as the needed first stage in applying for and gaining admittance to the Ecole.

The architectural section of the Ecole des Beaux-Arts to which Julia Morgan attended was not a monolithic institution located all in one place as the name might suggest. There were actually two places of learning, the Ecole and numerous individual ateliers. These two components each served with different but complementary roles and were joined in a rather remarkable manner. The Ecole's teaching function was limited to classroom lectures, the issuing of "architectural design problem" programs, holding examinations and judging student submissions called *concours* by which the student in a competitive format gained awards and points toward promotion. The judgments of student submissions were made in the form of a jury system, held behind closed doors, so that this element of process was not itself a part of the student's direct educational experience. The student or *eleve* of the academy attended lectures that consisted almost entirely of verbal presentations, hence limited to subjects communicable by words. Learning to design, which required graphic illustration, took place separately in a studio workshop called an atelier of an architectural master-patron whose primary focus was accordingly to develop and refine drawing skills. Prior to the Ecole's establishment, the Italian Renaissance had already brought about the change in the education-training format where the "workshop" for student learning as an "apprentor" was no longer "in the field" but had become an off-site "studio" where the master-practitioner would oversee the students' development of design abilities. The ateliers, however, were not the architectural offices (*agence*) of the masters; they were, in fact, private studio-schools of architecture, existing solely for teaching purposes overseen for a small fee by master-practitioners as patrons but entirely financially supported by the students. The attraction and value of the ateliers was twofold. They offered contact with an experienced and prominently successful "master-practitioner" providing guidance on the one hand, and the company of fellow students sharing learning and supporting each other in the production of presentation drawings, on the other. Students stridently sought the atelier of those master-patrons who had themselves won the ultimate Grand Prix de Rome at the Ecole, on the pragmatic assumption that they were the best guides to success in winning jury decisions and advancing their own careers.

The ateliers were all located in the neighborhood of the Ecole, in low-rent buildings with large enough spaces to accommodate the number of drawing-board tables needed. When the Royal Order of 1816 formally united the special schools of architecture, sculpture and painting into the "Ecole [Royal] de Beaux-Arts," in 1819 it relocated its quarters to a monastery building complex located on the Left Bank, appropriated and renovated for this purpose by the state. It was in this location at the time of Julia Morgan's attendance, and her atelier was within nearby walking distance.

The atelier was not administratively governed by the patron-master architect, but by a student, usually the most senior member elected to be the *massier*. The massier administered the collection of dues from the students and paid the rent, purchased coal for heat, fuel for lamps and the fees to the master-patron in charge of the atelier. The size of the ateliers varied considerably from several to over a hundred students. The patron would generally make visits to his atelier two or three times a week. The visits were conducted with formality and involved individual criticism and guidance to each of the students on their conceptions. The patron kept to himself the task of interviewing and accepting new applicants to his atelier. New applicants were usually introduced to the patron by letter of recommendation. An accepted student would upon arrival find a hierarchy of older and newer students; the newest would have to undergo an initiation. Atelier students were all men until the year Julia Morgan was accepted into the atelier of Marcel de Monclos. She was the first woman to have been granted admission since the beginning of the atelier as an institution.

The atelier first served to prepare a student for taking the admission examinations to the Ecole. The exams, after 1865, were given semiannually rather than annually. Aspirants could register and sit for any number of attempts limited only by being between fifteen to thirty years of age. The Ecole charged no tuition and was open to anyone except, by tradition, women, and foreigners were discouraged. In 1897 the tradition of not allowing women to enter the Ecole was changed by promulgated rule. That year, Julia Morgan became the first woman permitted to take the entrance examination.

The following description of the competitive training structure should illustrate the challenge and rigors of student life such as Julia Morgan faced while at the Ecole.

Design competitions, which began in a modest way from the earliest days of the academy, became the most important element of the Ecole's system. Competitions were the method by which students' designs were judged. It was the method by which students were awarded points, the accumulation of which led to promotion to higher class levels in the hierarchy of the system. After passing the entrance examination, an aspirant joined the second class level wherein the student must accumulate sixteen credit points based on being awarded "metals" or "mentions" for submissions. At this level, the points awarded are weighted according to subject area of training. Upon successfully gaining sixteen credit points, the student advanced to the first class level. This final level strictly focused on building design and the student was required to accrue ten credit points to achieve certification by the Ecole.

Competitive submissions took the form of two phases given in alternating sequence by the Ecole. The first was known as the *esquisses en loge* wherein students were assigned and confined to a small room (*en loge*) at the Ecole, and always alone to insure that their work was independent. They were allowed twelve hours to complete a design solution for some kind of architectural problem. The design concept the student created was set forth in a rough form of an idea sketch or *esquisse*. Upon the expiration of twelve hours, the student turned over the esquisse to an administrative guard, but was allowed to take a tracing paper copy of the submitted sketch with them. The second phase, known as the projects *rendus et atelier* ("completed projects"), permitted the student to return to his atelier with his tracing paper copy of his *esquisse*, in order to completely develop and synthesize his design in detail. This was achieved, usually with the assistance of fellow atelier counterparts, by the student himself fully illustrating the design solution with rendered plans, sections, elevations and perspective drawings. Since there was a strict time limit for these submissions, toward the end of these efforts a virtual frenzy broke out to complete and transfer all drawings from the atelier to the Ecole for the administrative guard to collect. The transfer of these large drawings was by cart (*charette*) usually pushed by a fellow student while the submitting student, along the way, continued putting finishing touches on them. The phrase to be *en charette* became the standard descriptive epitaph for describing last-minute delivery of architectural drawings. The jury would, among other things, compare the student's esquisse submission with his "completed project" submission, and if the latter departed from the earlier in any substantial way it could be thrown out of the competition for this reason alone.

In addition to these tasks, there were monthly competitions known as the *concours d'emulation* and grands concours, which were more advanced and difficult competitions for first class level students, and there was the one-time annual competition known as "the end of the year" event with the first prize being awarded to only one student. The prize was called Le Grand Prix de Rome. This award involved state financial support for one-year study in Rome and an assured state appointment as rewards. This was the ultimate achievement and honor for any aspirant. The first form of this annual prize was inaugurated in 1720. The monthly competitions had been later added mostly in response to the increasing number of students, but also served as preparation for "the end of the year" competition.

Because each student was permitted to progress at his or her own speed, they could enroll for every concours they wished to enter. In order to qualify for promotion, a student had to earn credit points in each of the curriculum subjects. But for a student to remain in the Ecole, they needed only to submit one or two *concours* a year at the minimum. If they did not do so they were dropped from the record and were required to take the admissions exams again. A student could participate in as many concours as they wanted or needed for promotion, limited only by coming to the age of thirty. Promotions did not occur at a prefixed time period. Students did not "graduate" in the fixed-schedule sense of the term, as this would be understood of educational systems in the United States. Historically, the Grand Prix de Rome, which could only be awarded to French citizen students, was the school's culmination stage for graduating one student per year. This was so until 1867 when a "diploma'" certificate system was additionally instituted together with the monthly *concours d'emulation* in response to the credential needs emerging at the time. Formal diplomas were not awarded to foreign students until 1887.

The jury for the competitions was usually made up of eight lifetime-appointed professors of the architectural section of the Ecole. They would decide which one, if any, among the student projects that were submitted was deserving of "mention" awards and which ones should receive the first, second and third prizes. The latter three awards were given in the form of "medals." The jury's selection decision was reported by the architectural section to the entire academy's professorial membership of painters, sculptures, musicians, among many others, for final judgment, and while this collective membership had the last word, it was unusual for this group not to concur with the recommendation of the architectural section.

While in her first atelier, at Marcel de Monclos's on the Rue de l'Ancien Comedie, to whom she had been guided by letter of introduction by Bernard Maybeck, Julia Morgan was informed that the Ecole would be allowing women to take the Beaux-Arts entrance examinations. At the time these examinations consisted, in part, of descriptive geometry, modeling, cast drawing, algebra, geometry, architectural history, theory of architecture, site planning and architectural design. Examination forms included both written and oral examinations.

The demanding intensity and stress of architectural student life in the atelier and especially at the Ecole began with these examinations. Writing to Lucy and Pierre LeBrun in July 1897, Julia Morgan described her ordeals of taking her first entrance examination:

"You are given from 8 am to 8 pm *en loge*. It was very hot weather and it was impossible to close an eye the night before, so I was up at five . . . and was down at the school a little after seven, as the head guard had said if I come early he would take me up before the men began to arrive, it being supposed there were two Americans to enter. But when I got there, it turned out the other was a myth. There was a single individual sitting with his drawing board at the base of the 'statue pillar' in the middle of the first court, and a guard who said they had made a mistake, and I would be let in last. So as people began to come, I went up to the quad and walked up and down and up, seeing the students arrive, in all sorts of regalia, by ones, in groups, until it seemed an almost endless time and number. It was nearly half past eight before things quieted down and one ventured back. I was put in a loge—a little 6 X 8 room in the roof of the part over the Secretary's office—there is a suite of perhaps 30 to 50 rooms up there. It had a table and stool and stove as furnishings, with a window out on the court of base-relief friezes with the fountains in the center. I did not notice particularly just then that the entire ceiling was skylight, with no way of covering it, but when the sun arrived a few minutes later, and looked through on your head all day with no escape, then, being an exceedingly hot day, you did notice, and the trickle of the water in the court below was aggravating—sort of insult to injury."[1]

She went on to describe how: "The program was very difficult for the 12 hours, for it had to be drawn very carefully. I was very tired, and got so nervous I absolutely could not keep the ink in the drawing pen or get a point on a pencil. In spite of that, I had my plan finished and the elevation about penciled by 4 'clock, when I took up the scale with a sudden suspicion, and found I had made a mistake calculating, as I cannot yet think in the meters, and the whole thing was too low, though in proportion. That just finished all hopes. I rubbed out the first story and simply put in the quickest and only thing I could—utterly bad—but it was eight and the guard there."[2] The examination having ended she returned to her lodgings at 10 Rue de Regard: "I went home and sat down on the sofa to rest a minute before dinner as I had not had a thing all day—and woke just as I was on coming in—at half past three in the morning."[3]

Yet another examination ordeal conveyed to the LeBrun's was the occasion upon which Julia Morgan was taking an oral examination in mathematics: "It's the most trying ordeal . . . and seems to depend more on the amount of nerve than of knowledge. There were thirteen examined before me the day I came up and everyone failed entirely; those big strong fellows would get up, tremble, turn white, clutch their hands, and seem to have no thinking power left at all. It seems very silly, but I think you would do the same; it seems a sort of contagion. Being the last on the list, I'd hoped to be almost alone, but probably from mischief though they were perfectly polite and gentlemanly, and have been throughout, the room kept filling up all the morning until when I was called there was a room full. I tried to pretend I was not afraid, and perfectly steady, and actually believed it until at the end of the first problem I discovered that my hand was rattling in the air, and the discovery surprised me, I could not do any more mathematics—it was enough for a pretty good mark, but you see, so many did nothing."[4]

Julia Morgan took entrance examinations in October 1897 and in April 1898 failing both times. She passed the examination in October 1898 ranking thirteenth out of hundreds of applicants, of which the Ecole accepted only thirty students of all those examined. Julia Morgan attended the Ecole from 1898 to 1901.

The atmosphere of atelier life was always hectic, calling for the occasional relief in tensions with pranks, hazing and the like. As the only woman in an atelier or at the academy, she was generally treated with courtesy, consideration and politeness by both teacher and student alike, perhaps out of deference. However, she was subject to the occasional harassment. But for Julia Morgan, what was worse was not to be taken seriously as an architectural candidate. She once wrote to Pierre LeBrun that one of her teachers "always seemed astonished if I do anything that shows the least intelligence." He would look over her work and say, "Ah, mais, c'est intelligent," as if it was not either required or expected to have such a capacity. Months later, however, Julia Morgan could report to her cousins about repeatedly going to the Beaux-Arts library to take out some book or other, discovering that "I'm getting a fine opinion of my good taste in books for I seldom pick out one but the library guards go look at it and come back with, 'Pas Possible [it is too valuable]!'"[5]

When M. Marcel de Monclos's atelier suffered a loss of students due to a lack of Grand Prix winners, his interest waned and he closed the atelier. At this point Julia Morgan chose to join the atelier of M. Benjamin Chasussemiche, himself the recipient of the 1890 Prix de Rome prize and the official architect of the city of Paris. Bernard Maybeck had also recommended Julia Morgan to him and he was willing to take her in. He was apparently motivated to do so by being attracted to the idea of possibly having charge of a women's atelier at the Ecole. Julia Morgan much preferred his personal style and temperament. Writing to LeBrun in 1898, she said of him: "He criticizes from an entirely different point of view from M. De Monclos, and it feels like a sort of weight has been lifted—and one could work in bigger, freer, happier way."[6]

The dominant theory and favored approach to the architectural design of buildings at the time of Julia Morgan's attendance at the Ecole was known as "academic eclecticism." The key concept is eclecticism, which meant to select and draw upon a particular historical "style" of architecture, i.e., to draw upon a style from the past and employ it to create a new building. The designer could "pick and choose" from the array of historical styles available, one that was felt to be appropriate to the building's purposes and problems facing him or her at present. The term "academic" in this phrase suggested that the designer had some appropriate discretionary latitude about how to compose and decorate the building subject to formalistic rules and principled methodological way. This aspect was also known as "academic classicism."

The methodological character of such an approach would be to begin the building's design by concentrating on the internal organization of a plan with each room appropriately related to the others according to their use or purpose. The rooms were to be arranged apriori on an axial or biaxial basis. The facades, generated as a consequence, would next be developed in symmetrical compositional terms with all architectural elements, such as doors and windows located to achieve a balance about the controlling vertical axis of bilateral symmetry. The facade was to be vertically divided in a tripartite format: base, middle and cap. All of this organization was usually accomplished in deference to some favored system of proportioning. The overall mass of the building was then embellished with decoration taken from multiple historical sources and imaginatively explored and adapted to the overall design. The major theorist and proponent of academic classicism teaching at the time was Jules Gaudet. Julia Morgan attended his lectures on architectural theory regularly, and on the occasion of Bernard Maybeck's visit to Paris in 1898, they attended Guadet's lectures together. She also took history of architecture courses from M. Bocowald and general history from M.

Lemmonier, all of whom she indicated she found very interesting and especially enjoyed.[7]

Julia Morgan accumulated the required sixteen points to complete the second class in less than two years after being accepted to the Ecole. She accrued the needed ten points to qualify for certification by gaining a first mention in her final submittal, for her thirtieth birthday was at hand. The Ecole's announcement came on February 4, 1902.

The Ecole des Beaux-Arts forged a considerable impression upon Julia Morgan's design sensibilities. She seems to have regarded the institution's major products to be the cultivation of taste and establishment of a regard for traditions. Some of the very notions about design offered by academic eclecticism and Guadet's theorizing directly appear in the buildings she designed for Asilomar, even though her approach to all the buildings in each case was in the Arts and Crafts style idiom, which will be considered next. Almost all of Asilomar's buildings, for example, have plans laid out with biaxial symmetry and the buildings' overall mass and facades reflect symmetrical organization of windows, doors and other features. These influences will be noted when we come to examine Julia Morgan's Asilomar buildings, artistically.

Julia Morgan, Ecole des Beaux Arts, Paris, 1889
(Identification Card Photo).

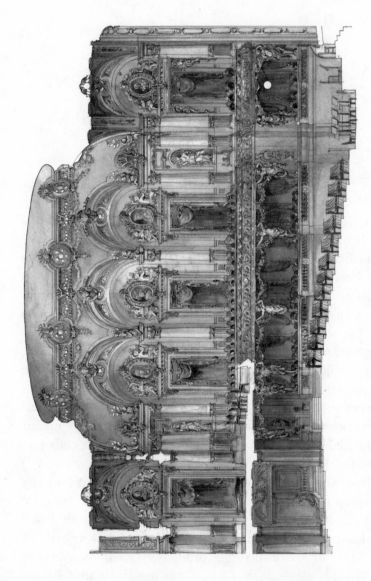

2.2 Julia Morgan's Palace Theater Design Submission, 1902 (Awarded 1st Prize Honors).

THE ARTS AND CRAFTS MOVEMENT: ENGLISH ORIGINS AND THE SAN FRANCISCO BAY REGION'S UNIQUE VERSION

Julia Morgan's buildings at Asilomar are generally identified with the design sensibilities inspired by the Arts and Crafts Movement. The phenomenon we call the Arts and Crafts Movement took its start in nineteenth-century Victorian Britain as a broad attempt to bring about a reunion of "life with labor and art with life". It was a diversely complex, non-homogeneous, somewhat conflicted movement, whose major motivations were combined in a two-sided quest for social and artistic reforms. The movement was a reactionary one whose targets were, the detrimental physical impact on the environment and the socially adverse effects generated by the Industrial Revolution, and the elaborate superficialities of the Victorian design habits. It stood as a call for reform, proposing how the productive and the consumptive sides of human life could be better related for greater overall benefit. It took the form of an ethically based aesthetic movement. It stood for the creation of an art that would be inclusive of things ordinary to common everyday life. In this view, artifacts were "not just disparate 'objects' made to be, in special moments, admired at leisure in rarified atmosphere with disinterested amusement on the one hand, nor on the other, to be intentionally mass produced, sold, used and discarded", but to be readily conceived, developed, utilized, maintained, preserved, enjoyed and admired. The movement strove to bind art imperatively to serving human wellbeing on a daily basis at many levels at once.

The preeminent personages that catalyzed the movement in England were A. W. N. Pugin, Thomas Carlyle, John Ruskin, William Morris and C. R. Ashbee. This group collectively represented the theoretical, polemical and activist force for the movement's general aims. The movement received its name in 1888 with the formation and founding show of "The Arts and Crafts Exhibition Society" in London. The "arts and crafts" phrase was first used and suggested by S. T. Cobden-Sanderson, a bookbinder and member of William Morris's Art Workers Guild from which the exhibition derived.

The Arts and Crafts Movement always accorded architecture a special place and role in the realization of its aims. The movement saw architecture as creating the larger setting by which other art forms and crafts could achieve the desired unification. As such, architects play a major role. Among the leading figures, as it developed in England, were A.W.N. Pugin, William R. Lethaby, Philip Webb, CFA Voysey, Mackay Hugh Bailey Scott, Charles Ashbee and Charles Rennie Mackintosh.

The Arts and Crafts Movement, with its overriding interest in harmony and the intrinsic value of all art, attempted to expand the idea of what should be considered as art. The movement wished to include in its range the applied and crafted arts as well as the fine arts. The chosen strategy to do so was by revising, if not dissolving, both the traditional categories and the hierarchical ordering of the arts into "higher or lower," "greater or lesser," "major or minor," "useful or decorative," "applied" or "fine" arts, in prevalent use at the time. The overarching interest was in realizing the unity of the arts. The traditional categorizations were thought of as negatively establishing social barriers and stimulating indifference or devaluation of the handcraft art forms.

The antecedent "aesthetic movement" from which the crafts movement emerged had already served to undermine the Western art tradition of categories and hierarchies. Approaching them from the newly found Oriental view and sensibilities, they were deemed "unnatural" distinctions. In these terms "everything" (from paintings to dining utensils) was to be elevated to and considered both fine and practical art.

The Arts and Crafts Movement's development in England and subsequently its spread in the European continent set the stage for its entry to the United States. Its entry on the Eastern seaboard had two important American influential links. Charles Eliot Norton, a close friend of John Ruskin and the first professor of fine arts at Harvard University, became the first president of the newly formed Arts and Crafts Society founded in 1897. Oscar Lovel Triggs, a professor at the University of Chicago, founded the Chicago Arts and Crafts Society in 1898. From these beginnings the spread and relative success of the Arts and Crafts Movement was accomplished by the efforts of a few major entrepreneurs such as Gustav Stickley, who among other things started his widely circulated Craftsman magazine in 1901, and Elbert Hubbard who started the Roycroft Shops enterprise. A major direct link was the English architect, Charles Ashbee, who was very instrumental in propounding the movement's ideas. As a frequent visitor to the United States, he devoted himself, mainly through lecture tours, to the theme of social reform through craft and the promotion of guilds.

Ernest A. Batchelder deftly and pointedly characterized this movement though with an Americanized slant in the Craftsman in 1909 as follows:

"It is doubtless a matter of common knowledge that the term 'arts and crafts' was coined by William Morris and his associates in London some twenty or more years ago for the immediate purpose of defining the nature of an exhibition that differed in one essential point from the conventional art exhibitions offered by the Royal Academy and similar institutions, which for many years had fostered the idea that the practice of art was the exclusive function of painters and sculptors. The unique feature of this exhibition was to be found in the fact that it sought to eliminate distinctions in art and furnish an opportunity for the display of work in wood, leather, glass, metal—in fact, any material adapted to artistic expression. The term 'arts and crafts' as it applied to this exhibition stood boldly for three things: It was a protest against the narrow and commonly accepted definition of art; it was a protest against the ugliness, the sham and pretense of a great portion of the English product of the day; it was a protest against the deplorable industrial conditions which that product represented. To put the matter into a positive statement, it sought to demonstrate the value of art combined with honest workmanship when applied to useful service; while it deplored the ugliness of the industrial product, it sought, not to withdraw art from it, but to bring art to it under the belief that an enduring basis for the appreciation of art must be established in the home rather than in the picture gallery; it sought to make manifest the dignity of labor and the individuality of the worker. On the strength of the ideals of which this exhibition was a concrete expression was formed the first society of arts and crafts. A seed from this parent tree fell upon American soil; it flourished, and has spread into a growth of remarkable proportions."[1]

The Arts and Crafts Movement was a major factor influencing the new form of architecture developing in the Bay Area in Julia Morgan's time, but in a unique way. The San Francisco Bay Region counts as one of the many manifestations of the Arts and Crafts Movement. The tie to the movement is evidenced by Charles Ashbee's visit to San Francisco in 1909 to give a talk at Stanford University on "The Arts and Crafts and the Spirit of Socialism." He at the time commented that the Bay Area exemplified the best realization sought for by the movement. Ashbee remarked, "Curious it is that the best work in the arts and crafts in America is already being produced on the West Coast." Like the arts and crafts movement in Britain, the San Francisco Bay Region began as a reaction to the Victorian design superficiality of the day and sought to improve the quality of its architecture and the quality of living environment. It did not have the same motivations, interest or intensity for social reform as the British movement, likely because it was too busy forming itself into being a society in the first place. Nor was the local movement antithetical to industrialization and machine production. Bay Area designers did not wholly or literally adopt the Arts and Crafts Movement, but were conditioned by other forces, interests and experiences. Among these were the hazardous side of nature such as earthquakes and fires, the mild climate and dramatic views, the mountainous terrain, the availability of local material resources, new technological developments, an adventurous and experimental mood, and the beginning of the naturalist movement as well as interest taken in early regional building history of the Indian and the Spanish Mexican eras.

The Arts and Crafts—oriented architecture in the San Francisco Bay Region is usually credited to Joseph Worcester, a Swedenborgian minister and amateur architect who, after traveling earlier to the area, left Boston in 1869 to settle in San Francisco. In 1876 he designed and built his home in the East Bay's Piedmont Hills overlooking the bay. In this house he

utilized unpainted shingles for all the exterior walls and roof
sheathings, and unpainted wide redwood boards for the entire
interior finishing. The roof support beams were left exposed.
There were no adornments and no historical ornamentation.
There were Spanish features to the design, such as outdoor
sleeping porch, trellises and large extended roof overhangs.
This house was to serve as the initial inspiration for the ethos
of the simple life and what was the precursor to the ideal of
"the simple home." Worcester's inspiration for the house is
believed to have come while accompanying John Muir on a
trip to Yosemite Valley. Seeing the many miner's cabins built in
a simple, direct and forthright manner instilled in him a desire
to build a house that would almost be a thing of nature—nature
being for him as an ecclesiastic, a work of God.

In the late 1880's on into the 1990's there arrived several
academically trained architects from the East Coast and
England in search of better opportunities for practicing their
art. Principal among them were A. Page Brown, Albert
Schweinfurth, Ernest Coxhead, Willis Polk, Louis Mullgardt,
John Hudson Thomas, Bernard Maybeck and John Galen
Howard. Julia Morgan, the only native-born figure and the
youngest, returned from Paris to join this group in 1902.

The group, while having many views in common, held to no
single or uniform doctrine of design, had no particular leader,
did not formally organize or become a school, but were
contemporaries, casually linked by friendships, tastes and ideas,
practicing architecture individually, each according to their own
instincts. This group drew upon several historical sources, not
only the Arts and Crafts Movement but also variously the Queen
Anne style, the Viennese Secession, the Art Nouveau, the Swiss
Chalet, and the Japanese Temple from Europe and Asia, the
Shingle style from the East Coast, the local Pueblo Indian and
Spanish Mission vernaculars and the Alpine lodges and log cabin,
as well as barn construction to be found in the immediate region.

In 1894 Joseph Worcester commissioned A. Page Brown
to design the Church of the New Jerusalem in San Francisco.
This church quickly gained a reputation and became the
symbol of the path that architecture and the handcrafts lifestyle
would take for the next decades. A. Page Brown had come to
San Francisco in 1889 from New York, where he had worked
for the firm of McKim, Mead & White, to open his own
practice. Participating in the design of the church were Albert
Schweinfurth and Bernard Maybeck, who was a draftsman in
Brown's office in 1890-91. Maybeck was born in New York,
the son of a woodcarver and he served an apprenticeship in
the same vocation. He had an early familiarity with and an
interest in English architecture and England's Arts and Crafts
Movement's design ideas. Maybeck lived for a time near
Worcester's Piedmont home and was favorably impressed by
it. Maybeck undertook, upon setting up his own office, to
design a house for the author, Charles Keeler, his first client,
in 1894. The design was influenced by Worcester's house,
but was developed with much more sophistication in
conception and treatment and included some unprecedented
features. Notable was leaving the entire structural system of
the house exposed throughout the interior. Maybeck's house
for Keeler drew considerable attention and gained even more
widespread familiarity when Keeler wrote and published his
widely read book in 1904, inspired by the house, entitled
The Simple Home, which he dedicated to Maybeck.[2]

Maybeck studied at the Ecole in Paris from 1882 to 1886,
in the atelier of Jules André. André was known for his
rationalist approach to architecture, emphasizing the
expression of structure. He was also interested in landscape
design and the relationship of building to the environment.

Maybeck became a major figure in the local Arts and
Crafts tradition of the Bay Region but nevertheless remained,
even in this connection, a rather eccentric and eclectic

architect. Julia Morgan and Maybeck maintained an active friendship over their careers, exchanging ideas and sometimes working together on projects. They were to be honored together by the University of California, Berkeley, receiving ceremonial "Doctorate of Laws" degrees in May 1929. Julia Morgan's honorary degree read as follows:

"Distinguished alumna of the University of California; Artist and Engineer; Designer of simple dwellings and stately homes, of great buildings nobly planned to further the centralized activities of her fellow citizens; Architect in whose work harmony and admirable proportions bring pleasure to the eye and peace of mind."

Julia Morgan's projects were designed in the "arts and crafts" vernacular quantitatively more than any other specific style. This approach was taken for the majority of the numerous residential commissions, particularly in Berkeley, California, where it was favored. Simplicity, utility and economy were the goals of the Arts and Crafts architectural movement, and much of Julia Morgan's work is reflective of these principles in overall design. Her most brilliant exercise of the Arts and Crafts idiom was the design of St. John's Presbyterian Church in a residential neighborhood at 2640 College Avenue in Berkeley. It was completed in 1910 and brought Julia Morgan a considerable reputation for achieving so much architectural expression for what was even then considered to be absurdly little cost.

Julia Morgan's architecture at Asilomar manifests much of what the Arts and Crafts Movement proposed and stood for, particularly the adoption of the local uses of form, rusticity of materials, and the blending of colors and textures with those native to the site. The larger extent of this influence will be seen when we examine the artistic considerations of Julia Morgan's buildings at Asilomar.

Church of The New Jerusalem, San Francisco, Constructed 1894.

Church of The New Jerusalem, San Francisco
(View toward front altar).

THE SAN FRANCISCO BAY REGION: EMERGING TECHNOLOGIES AND INSTITUTIONS IN THE FORMATIVE YEARS

Julia Morgan's architectural career and accomplishments were afforded an opportunity for realization by certain antecedent events that occurred in the San Francisco Bay Region, which she necessarily drew upon in the course of her work. Needless to say the practice of architecture is greatly dependent on the availability of materials, the existing technologies and construction techniques and the influence of financial and governing institutions constituting a "milieu" for its exercise.

The San Francisco Bay Region, from the time of the Gold Rush to the early decades of the twentieth century, underwent enormous and dramatic changes by virtue of population, institutions and technologies that arrived on the scene and impacted the built environment. This was the unique and intense period that saw an immense increase in the area's population from 166,500 in 1850 to over 560,000 by 1870, three-quarters of whom lived in the immediate Bay Area. It generated an immense need for new buildings, the rise of new rural settlements and the increased density of urban cities. It involved inclusively, the transition from pre-industrial to industrial technologies and practices; the growth of economic middle and upper classes; the advent of large corporations, industries and commercial companies; the growth of conscious concern for the implications of the fire and earthquake hazards of nature; the instituting of legal regulations for governing building design and construction; institutional formalization of professionalism; entrepreneurial and academic experimentalism; innovation of new construction materials and techniques; the organization and training of labor skills and the development of public sector infrastructure for servicing individual buildings and interconnecting communities.

The Gold Rush attracted people of different races, talents and skills to Northern California. About 90 percent came from the Eastern seaboard, the rest mainly from England, Ireland, Canada, Italy, Germany, Russia and China. While this sudden arrival of people affected all sides of life, it particularly overwhelmed the capacity of the region to accommodate the vast need for housing and other sorts of buildings. At the beginning stages in 1849, people resorted to temporary or makeshift solutions to satisfy their immediate need for shelter. These shelters were crudely made, mostly by non-professionals and almost always in wood scavenged, cannibalized or appropriated from various "at hand" sources, including the dismantling of ships. The situation was characterized in the following way: "Every material that could be used in the building of tents, houses and stores became of immense value, commanding any price which might be suggested by the unscrupulous spirit of speculation . . . muslins, calicoes, canvas, old sails, brush, logs, boards, iron, zinc, tin, adobes and boxes all were employed in constructing some kind of 'building,' either for shelter or a place to carry on trade."[1] The results were dense collections of shacks, shanties, lean-to's, cabins and barns of all sorts, sizes and qualities. Even the multitude of ships that lay anchored in San Francisco bay were often modified and became warehouses and living accommodations during this period.

The intense demand for housing caused builders of this period to begin to turn to materials and building methods produced by industrial techniques. Precut materials and prefabricated buildings in great numbers were imported to the Bay Area by ship from manufacturers, not only from the Eastern seaboard, but from as far as Australia and New Zealand. The need for importing housing by ship began to be offset in the 1850s with the development of local capacity for producing materials. Lumber was the first building material produced locally with the construction of mechanized sawmills in such places as Redwood City, Oakland, Marin and Placerville, for milling redwood logs that were plentiful in the coastal forest ranges of Northern California. The circular and vertical saw machines were introduced by 1860. Alvinza Howard, originally a mining tycoon, developed an enormous lumber production and distribution system in the region that utilized such devices as flumes to transport logs and John Dolbeer's 'Donkey Steam Engine' which Dolbeer invented in 1881, to haul logs off mountains to the mills on a tram system.[2] This invention alone made a greater amount of wood available at very low cost.

The traditional form of building with wood in the region was called "brace frame" construction. This consisted of heavy post and beam timbers, split from logs by hand and connected by means of mortise and tenon joints. Each member had to be individually shaped for the particular location within the overall building system. The frame once completed, was then sheathed with various kinds of boards. This type of construction became easier and speedier with the mechanization of the sawmilling process that permitted qualitatively better preparation and more accurately shaped lumber for joining together.

However, this method of wood construction was replaced over time by the introduction of a form of construction developed in the Midwest in the 1830s called "balloon frame" construction. It was invented by Augustine Taylor, a carpenter from Connecticut in 1833 for construction of a church in Chicago. The name is derived from the derision given the invention by the then orthodox brace frame builders, who felt this type of construction would literally blow away "like balloons." The system utilized standard dimensional lumber, produced from newly introduced, mechanized planing mills capable of accurately dressing the faces and edges of various lumber sizes and lengths, which were then assembled with forged metal nails. The wall framing was made almost entirely from one size of lumber known as the two-by-four-inch stud wall that extended from the foundation continuously up to the roofline. An improved variant of this system, called the Western platform frame, was being used in the San Francisco Bay Region by the 1900s. This method allowed each floor level of more than one-story building to be constructed upon and supported by each lower floor level. Wood boards or shingles were installed as sheathing. This balloon frame system proved stronger, lighter, easier, more flexible and speedier to build, so much so that it is still in nationwide use to this day. These same planing mills brought about the capacity to produce locally, prefabricated wood doors and windows and their frames, all of which could be custom ordered ready made. Window glass was being locally produced by a glassworks, originally set up by an entrepreneur Charles Kohler, in 1863.

Wood construction, however, had a downside. Fire posed a widespread danger. Almost all settlements in the region, from Monterey to Sacramento, fell victim to major fires, particularly in the early 1850s. It was about this time that urban city cores were rebuilt with more fire-resistant materials, mostly brick. Here again, because of the lack of local abilities for production, brick, stone and iron materials were imported by ship until local clay and stone deposit sites were uncovered.

The production of brick was limited until the continuous kiln system of firing clay was introduced in the 1880s that greatly improved capacity to produce high quality bricks. The use of quarried stone was not economically viable until railroad distribution systems were constructed during the 1870s. The concern over the numerous fires provoked municipal governments, with considerable pressure from insurance companies, to create building construction and zoning fire laws, the first of which was passed in San Francisco in 1850.

While brick structures resisted fires far better than wood, they were found to be vulnerable to the earthquake. Balloon-framed wood structures generally suffered little, if any, major damage from earthquakes. Earthquakes, particularly those of 1865 and 1868, did substantial damage to structures, especially masonry buildings with load-bearing brick walls. Engineers, architects and builders, who became conscious of the problem, searched for building improvements and proposed new methods for earthquake-resistant construction. The three decades toward the end of the nineteenth century saw much experimentation by entrepreneurial inventors who played a major role in developing new construction techniques that improved the strength and fire resistance of buildings. Among those proposed for brick was William H. Foye's 1869, patented method of reinforcing masonry walls with grids of vertical and horizontal metal called "bond iron." Structural iron was introduced into American building construction, by William Strickland, in Philadelphia in 1822. Iron, both structural and decorative, was manufactured in the Bay Area as early as 1853. The Union Iron Works Co. was established by Peter Donahue in San Francisco in 1860. But the structural use of iron in buildings was found to be vulnerable, as was steel, when exposed to fire. Many methods developed to encase these materials with others, such as non-load bearing brick, stone or terra cotta, in order to be more fire resistive. Best for being both fire resistive and earthquake resistive were structures constructed in concrete. The most notable innovations in this material were made by the builder inventor Ernest L. Ransome of the Pacific Stone Company, who patented designs for reinforcing concrete with square but spirally twisted iron reinforcing bar in 1884. The first major architectural use of this technology was to be applied in the Leland Stanford Junior Museum building at Stanford University in 1889.

Steel frame buildings performed well, particularly against collapse in earthquakes, but suffered from fire damage depending for the most part on the type of protective cladding used. With the advent of large service corporations and commercial stores needing large amounts of open floor space to be built on the smallest amount of land, the multi-storied steel frame building became the prototypical solution. These were clad in non-load bearing stone, brick and eventually with terra cotta veneering for fire protection and appearance interests. The tall office building type was first developed in Chicago. However, with business expanding rapidly in the Bay Area, by the end of the 1870s the administrative and service needs of the emerging enterprises began to be housed in highrise office buildings. In the case of San Francisco these buildings were concentrated in a zoned district of the city called the "Downtown." The high rise made its first appearance in San Francisco with Michael de Young's ten-story Chronicle newspaper building in 1888, designed by the Chicago architect Daniel Burnham. Many high-rise buildings, such as the Mills, Chronicle and Merchant buildings among others that were built in the 1880s with iron and steel frames using riveted joints and, ranging from six to fifteen stories in height, all were structurally designed for resisting wind forces only. A notable exception was the San Francisco Call newspaper building that incorporated a system of diagonal steel bracing specifically designed to resist earthquake stresses as well as wind forces.

Multistory buildings could not function without gas or electric lighting, running hot and cold water supply, flush toilets, steam or water heating, elevators or telephones. And all of these internal building systems depended upon the creation of a broad infrastructure. A distribution system of street paths, transportation, communication and utility services had to be provided. These services were all constructed in the forms of stone and concrete sidewalks, cobblestone and tarmac-covered streets, public transportation by means of streetcars and cable cars (the latter invented by A. Hallidie, a metal wire rope manufacturer located in San Francisco) were constructed. The transcontinental telegraph, which began in 1858 utilizing Samuel Morse's patent of 1837, had developed into the Western Union Co. by 1860. The telephone and electric power, underground sewer, gas and water pipe lines were all developed in the decades of the emerging "skyscraper" buildings. The first commercial electrical distribution system in the United States was created in San Francisco by the Pacific Lighting Company, a power and fuel enterprise. The first construction of reinforced concrete sidewalks with basement level vaults which incorporated delivery elevator service equipment and light letting glass block, were two examples of the innovations occurring in the 1880s and 1890s. These factors introduced a dramatically new appearance to the built "downtown" environment to which Julia Morgan visited, on a regularly basis, in the years of her youth. Domestic architecture, in contrast with commercial buildings, continued to be constructed in wood and while incorporating new infrastructure services and devices, eclectically adopted, for the most part, the Victorian fashion of form and ornamentation, the latter decorative elaborations being now made by "machine carving" technologies into wood patterns and shapes of all sorts as features.

A major force contributing to and supporting these events was the development and construction of the transcontinental

railroad system. The realization of the system was energized
by Theodore Judah, a railroad engineer, entrepreneur and
promoter who developed a plan for a feasible overland line
and who himself planned the western route to and within
California. Frustrated in a longtime effort to gain financial
support for his scheme, in 1861 he convinced a group of
successful Sacramento merchants to invest. This group
consisted of Charles Crocker, Mark Hopkins, Collis
Huntington and Leland Stanford who would eventually come
to be known, due to their great wealth and influence, as "The
Big Four." These men, along with Cornelius Cole, all-powerful
political activists, organized the state's Republican Party in
1856. Given their investment interest, they successfully
lobbied for the passage of the Pacific Railway Act of 1862,
which made land available for the construction of the
transcontinental railroad into the state. Theodore Judah died
in 1863, at the age of 37 years. In that same year "The Big
Four" created an independent "dummy" construction
company named the Southern Pacific Company to support
constructing the Central Pacific Railway. The Central Pacific
joined the Union Pacific with the last spike being driven on
May 10, 1869, to complete the transcontinental connection.

By 1870 the Southern Pacific Company had become a
"giant" having gained strategic control over basically all
transportation in and out of California, virtually having a
monopolistic grip over the state's interstate commerce. In
1803 Charles Crocker formed the Crocker, Woolworth &
Co. and the National Bank of San Francisco, later headed
by his son William Crocker and renamed Crocker Bank,
substantially to provide another source of investment funds
in relation to the Southern Pacific Co. The Pacific
Improvement Company was formed as a subsidiary of both
the Southern Pacific Co. and the Central Pacific Co., in about
1869, as a "landholding" company to manage various
property developments, particularly in California. This

company was headed by W. E. Brown, who also was vice president of Crocker Bank.

Military facilities and industrial buildings built from the mid-1850s were designed by professionally trained engineers, most of who were trained as military and civil engineers at such schools as West Point and Cornell University in the East and the University of California and Stanford University in the Bay Area. The phrase "civil engineer" was first used in 1763 by the English engineer, John Smeaton, to distinguish civil from military practices. Structures by these trained engineers put the solutions to problems of the structural design of facilities on an empirical (experimentally tested) and mathematically rationalized basis. Such training efforts and the increase of scientific and technical knowledge inaugurated and increased refinement, professionalization, standardization and regulation of building construction, changing the way buildings were built and the way they looked in the late nineteenth and early twentieth centuries.

The Mechanics Lien Law was first enacted in 1850 to protect construction labor and material suppliers from nonpayment. By 1901 a law was passed, mandating that architects in California could not practice without a license granted by the state. Activity to establish a state education system resulted in the University of California Legislative Act of 1866 creating the university, which opened in 1869 with agriculture, mining and mechanical colleges. In 1903 the University of California at Berkeley established a School of Architecture with a curriculum of formal courses to add to the already existing School of Civil Engineering. The local chapter of the American Institute of Architects and the San Francisco Society of Architects increased their members and gained greater influence over the practices and regulations having to do with buildings. A professional journal, The Architect and Engineer of California, was founded in 1905, circulating information on new technologies, new building projects and theoretical discussions among practitioners. The office of the state architect, whose purpose (among other things) was to provide objective and uniform standards for the building industry, was established in 1907. These events, together with the increased frequency of updating building codes and regulating building designs, constituted a dramatic era of change.

Julia Morgan's formative years coincided with a great many of these technical and institutional developments. Growing up and maturing during much of this period allowed her to witness firsthand the appearance not only of new technological innovations occurring in the built environment of the region but also the new architectural forms. Julia Morgan opened her architectural office in the Merchant Building, then one of the city's taller "skyscrapers." This building was a product of the formation of the Merchant Exchange in 1850 for centralizing trading operations in San Francisco, the state's chief commercial center.

Julia Morgan's interest in materials and technologies was manifested from the earliest of her working career when she recommended the use of the latest developments in steel-reinforced concrete material for the Hearst Mining and Greek Theater projects she helped design while working for John Galen Howard. She used the same material for her bell tower and library projects at Mills College. She was the first architect to design and construct a concrete house in the hills of Berkeley. Even while in Paris she received journals containing technical articles about latest developments, and one of her favorite publications, while in independent practice, were the journal Architect & Engineer, which reported on and presented much information about materials, structural design and construction techniques for architectural projects. While Julia Morgan was herself competent and capable of engineering, she was much too busy to undertake to do that element of design work and left this to others on her staff or consultants. Walter Huber was her chief engineer and did all her structural steel design work. Walter Steilberg, himself an architect and engineer, did almost all of her concrete and timber structural design work either as a staff member in her office or as an independent consultant. Since Julia Morgan was much concerned with the craft of building, she was fervent about doing almost all field inspections of construction work on the site of each of her projects herself. Before giving her approval, she knew and reviewed every detail to assure that the constructed work conformed to what was needed and she intended.

Julia Morgan utilized relatively little steel frame construction in her work. She preferred concrete. "She liked the idea that [i.e.,concrete] was the structure, and the other [i.e., steel frame] structure wasn't hiding somewhere in the closet."[3] She did not think steel was of itself an architecturally expressive material. The vast majority of her work was in wood or concrete in both of which she took considerable technical interest. Wood, especially redwood, was plentiful and inexpensive in the Bay Region. The logging industry, as we have seen, was making refined lumber readily available for constructing buildings. As a native of the Bay Area, Julia Morgan was virtually "born" to understanding the nature, virtues and limits of this material. While the early stages of the development of concrete as a construction material, found primarily in industrial buildings, had begun in the Bay Region, particularly by Ernest Ransome in the 1880s, this material was scarcely used as a fully architectural aesthetic and expressive material until the Stanford Museum was built in 1889 as mentioned earlier.

It may have been in Paris where Julia Morgan gained insight into the nature of concrete, especially its architectural value as well as its technical virtues. August Perret (1872-1954), a contemporary of Julia Morgan, was a prominent figure in Paris, as an innovative architect-constructor dedicated to the development and use of concrete as a fully architectural material. Perret attended the Ecole des Beaux-Arts from 1891 to 1893. He left the Ecole without gaining a "diplome" in order to start his own architectural-construction firm, which included his two brothers, Claude and Gustave. Julia Morgan was in Paris from 1896 to 1902 and would have certainly come to know about August Perret's innovative explorations in the use of steel-reinforced concrete as a new architectural idiom.[4] August Perret was socially and culturally active, a prominent figure among the artistic elite and noted in the publications of the day. His buildings stirred admiration as well as controversy. Unlike August Perret, Julia Morgan did not hold to the exclusive use of concrete for all of her buildings nor to the view of "academic classicism" for her architectural imaging of buildings. But there are significant parallels between them that are worthy of note. Both were exposed to the intellectual heritage of the French Rationalist view in the vein of the medieval structuralist, Viollet le Duc (1814-1879), followed by Auguste Choisy (1841-1909) and Julian Gaudet (1834-1908) at the Ecole. Both took classes from, and much admired, Julien Guadet while at the Ecole and both were committed to the idea that good architecture is a result of good construction, i.e., they rejected the notion that design could be separated from execution, as pure academicism would have it. They both appreciated the values of the medieval system where architecture was shaped by craftsmen, actively solving technical problems of structure and construction at the building sites. Both Julia Morgan and August Perret spent much of their time overseeing the installation of work at the job site. Both were extraordinary in their interest in structure as a source of architectural expressiveness. They also shared together the embracement of new technology with a sense of historicity, i.e., the architect was responsible for sustaining social "continuity" and thus mediated between the past and the present, between innovation and conservatism. They both shared a lack of understanding of and dislike for the then evolving "modernism" and avant-garde enthusiasts.

While August Perret and Julia Morgan were avid about architecture being a "craft," Julia Morgan differed in her employment of concrete technology, subordinating it to more diverse eclectic artistic aims than Perret's singular "classicism." They shared a sense of the necessity of craft discipline to realize cultural sophistication in architectural forms. Some insight into how Julia Morgan, in her own case, undertook to achieve this end, may be accessed by comparing two of her major projects, to which we now turn.

The Merchants Exchange Building, San Francisco, 1906 aftermath.
(Julia Morgan's office location from 1907 to 1950)

John Dolbeer's "Donkey Steam Engine", at work in 1890.

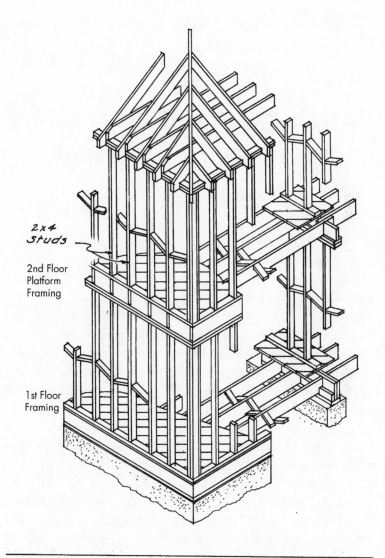

2x4 studs

2nd Floor Platform Framing

1st Floor Framing

WESTERN (or PLATFORM) FRAMING

Illustration of Western Platform Framing.

JULIA MORGAN'S TWO LARGEST PROJECTS: HEARST CASTLE AND ASILOMAR,

A COMPARISON

The Hearst family was the source of Julia Morgan's two largest and most complex projects. The Asilomar Conference Grounds commission was given to her by the YWCA, the actual contractual client for the project, but indirectly the appointment came at the request of Mrs. Phoebe Hearst, who had herself conceived the idea of creating a permanent YWCA summer meeting place and had offered funds and other kinds of support, for the conference grounds including the first needed building. This is the building that became the Phoebe Apperson Hearst Social Hall, now the administration building, at Asilomar. Given the previous services provided by Julia Morgan for Mrs. Hearst, for example the remodeling of her "Hacienda" residence in Pleasanton and "Wyntoon," her vacation residence in Mt. Shasta, together with Mrs. Hearst's admiration of Julia Morgan's abilities while working for John Galen Howard on the designs for the Mining Building at the University of California at Berkeley, she clearly thought of Julia Morgan as the most suitable and qualified professional architect for designing the project.

Over time, as further Asilomar building needs arose and funding became available, Julia Morgan continued to be appointed by the YWCA as the architect for each new facility. But this was likely also due, at least in part, to other previously established relationships. For example, Julia Morgan had, early upon opening her independent architectural practice, designed a small cottage located in Pebble Beach, Monterey, for Grace Fisher Richards, who was also a Kappa Alpha Theta sorority sister at the University of California, Berkeley. Ms. Richards was a chairperson on various local YWCA committees, including one that related to Asilomar, and eventually was appointed as the director of the Oakland Chapter of the YWCA. Ms. Richards, in that role, called upon Julia Morgan to be the architect for the new Oakland YWCA building that was later completed in 1913.

The commission to be the architect for the Hearst Castle or "La Cuesta Encantada" (The Enchanted Hill) in San Simeon was also the product of an already established relationship with Mrs. Phoebe Hearst's son, William Randolph Hearst. While working for John Galen Howard on the Greek Theater at the University of California, Berkeley, Julia Morgan met William Randolph Hearst, who had traveled from New York to visit his mother. Upon meeting him, Julia Morgan found Mr. Hearst quite conversant with the arts, including architecture, and they found other common interests, including an ardent love of California landscape. At the end of this visit, Mr. Hearst commented that he would someday have a commission for her; thereby indicating already at this stage in his life, that he had a vision or "dream" for building upon what was referred to then as "The Ranch."

Since these two architectural projects were the two largest, most complex and longest enduring endeavors of Julia Morgan's professional career, comparing them with each other can be a source of insights into her client relations abilities and design talents.

Despite Mrs. Phoebe Apperson Hearst's initial influential role, the YWCA was, for Julia Morgan, an institutional client of very modest means, for the most part, relying on patrons and gifts, and having fairly definite needs with respect to buildings. On the other hand, William Randolph Hearst represented a client of enormous wealth with vague and amorphic wishes that perpetually shifted. William Randolph Hearst was an amateur architect, actively involved at every stage, himself conjuring up design images and presenting them to the architect for consideration of inclusion or revision of existing work. On the other hand, the YWCA Asilomar executive committee gave to Julia Morgan a free hand to develop building designs on her own, more or less limiting its engagement to decisions for final approval. For Julia Morgan these two clients represented two very different motivations with two different visions and vastly different financial economies to which she would serve for a number of years. William Randolph Hearst was a singular individual and personal client; the YWCA was an institutional entity with multiple board and committee members, along with building donor patrons, as a client.

Phoebe Apperson Hearst died in April 1919 at the age of seventy-six. She was a longtime widow of George Hearst, who had become wealthy in the Gold Rush. Mrs. Hearst spent many decades as a philanthropist primarily in support of education, women and children interests. At the time of Mrs. Hearst's final illness, Julia Morgan had written to thank her for all the many years of support and kindness "since those Paris days when you were so beautifully kind to a most painfully shy and homesick girl," referring to a visit together in Paris that had occurred over twenty years past. William Randolph Hearst had returned from New York, where he had become a wealthy publishing magnate, to be with his mother during her illness. Upon her passing, having inherited the

family fortune to add to his own, he visited Julia Morgan at
her office in San Francisco one morning in that same year, to
announce that he had a project in mind and she was his choice
to be his architect.

The project was to construct a bungalow at a site atop
the highest westerly peak (1600 feet above sea level) of his
270,000 acre estate. The estate consisted of land that his
father had begun purchasing in 1865, located in the Santa
Lucia Mountains, about five miles inland from a small harbor
and fishing village named San Simeon at the edge of the
Pacific Ocean. "Miss Morgan," he reportedly said, "I would
like to build something up on the hill at San Simeon. I get
tired of going up there and camping in tents. I'm getting a
little old for that. I would like to get something that would be
more comfortable."[1] He had with him a used book he had
purchased containing an example of a type of "bungalow"
ranch house he had in mind, but as they conversed Julia
Morgan, already familiar with his art interests, began within a
very short time to realize that more than a small bungalow
was going to be in play. Before he left the office that day, the
conception had already shifted from that of a modest
bungalow; in fact they both laughed at the idea. At the very
next meeting the basic idea had become a "castle like"
structure that would serve both as a residence and a museum.
Subsequently, it became a large complex of buildings to serve
his social appetite as well. It was, in concept, to be a group of
buildings with a towered main structure that would collectively
resemble a "Spanish hill town." Aptly described, in summary,
by James Cary: "Hearst's Castle would become America's
most flamboyant and ostentatious architectural gesture, a 144-
room celebrity playground where Hollywood stars such as
Greta Garbo and Charlie Chaplin would gather to relax. And
it would gain mythical status as the mansion, Xanadu, featured
in Orson Welles's 1941 cinema classic, Citizen Kane."[2]

William Randolph Hearst's motivations were complex—as Julia Morgan very well had sensed—including a display of his social status for "mansion building", and in this he was following the Vanderbilts, Deerings and Astors. His lifelong enthusiasm for art collecting, a desire to leave a legacy, and his childhood bond with a place he dearly loved, together with his sense of theatricality, all coalesced into a single building dream, then into an actual event; what William Randolph Jr. labeled "The Magnificent Obsession." Reflective of his enthusiasm, William Randolph Hearst once remarked to his son, Randolph Jr., about this hilltop site at San Simeon, "I love it. I just love it."[3]

Given the twenty-three years of their architect-client relationship, it is most interesting to note at the outset, that William Randolph Hearst Jr. described his father in his family biography, as "In many ways . . . a medieval man."[4] The architect and engineer Walter Steilberg, a consultant to and long associated with Julia Morgan's office, in an interview, said of her, "I think Julia Morgan was strictly a medieval architect."[5] These two disparate remarks may be a clue to their comradeship, to the steadfast, though often headstrong, working relationship they developed in the course of designing and constructing Hearst Castle. They at times kidded each other with bouts of laughter, about being "fellow architects", comrades by virtue of a project. As two willing protagonists, William Randolph Hearst Jr. described their relationship in full vibrancy:

"If my father was crazy to undertake the project, so was Julia Morgan, a tiny but strong-willed woman who was bold enough to agree with his vision and accept the job as architect." "She wore horn-rimmed glasses and usually dressed in tailor-made suits with handmade Parisian blouses. Always prim and proper, she topped her understated yet distinctive garb with a trim, dark hat affectionately called the Queen

Mary style. Underneath that impeccable attire and highly
professional air were a steel-trap mind and a will of iron." "I
used to listen to her and the old man, go at it in her small
office at the top of the hill. She and Pop had some real
squawks, let me tell you, but both were so formal and low-
keyed that an outsider would hardly have noticed. Indeed,
through all the years she always called him "Mister Hearst"
and he referred to her as "Miss Morgan." At the end of most
discussions she deferred to him as the client. But not without
forcing my father to consider all the questions in her mind,
the cost, and the new architectural problems created." "She
managed to cajole, plea, demand, and warn Pop in the most
courteous, professional language. However, if one read
carefully between the lines, she caught the old man up short
many a time and indicated she would not retreat on her view
unless he had a darn good answer. Several times their views
were so far apart that Julia quit, but pop simply would not
hear of it. They would come to some kind of compromise,
and she would soon be drawing a new sketch. Julia was as
totally committed to the project as my father. The two had
an extraordinary adventure together."[6]

Walter Steilberg offered his impression that "Miss Morgan
and Mr. Hearst had this in common . . . they were both long-
distance dreamers. That didn't mean that they necessarily
had the same dreams, but they were looking way, way
ahead."[7] Both envisioned the project to someday be a public
museum.

It is indicative of the times in which she worked, that the
documentary film production of the construction of the Hearst
Castle, which has been shown for several decades and
regularly so at the Hearst Castle public tour building theater,
refers to Julia Morgan, in its audio script, mistakenly, as William
Randolph Hearst's secretary. It seems warranted to infer from
what is known that Julia Morgan was able to work for and

with individual and institutional clients alike with considerable evenness of temperament, equal dedication and relative ease.

In comparing these two markedly different projects, Hearst Castle and Asilomar, several contrasts seem pertinent. The two site plans reveal Julia Morgan's respective responses to her distinctively different clients and to the different implications of the natural sites themselves. The San Simeon site of Hearst Castle is at the crown of a very steep hill, the land dropping sharply away from its apex on all sides, whereas Asilomar's site is virtually a level plane with very gentle slopes within its borders. The very arrangement of San Simeon and Asilomar's buildings and their functions respond each in their different ways to their respective site's natural terrain and the activities to be accommodated.

At San Simeon, Julia Morgan developed a classical, axially controlled Beaux-Arts site plan, with an Italianate demeanor, responding to both the steep slopes and the expansive views to be afforded from each building. The Hearst's private quarters housed in the massive main building, named "La Casa Grande," sits at the very center of the circular or oval site plan arrangement of other buildings and improvements, and at the high point of a terraced layout. Thus, La Casa Grande dominates all the other structures. In descending order, as the land drops away down the hillside, on the next terrace level there are located the guest buildings, Casa del Mar, Casa del Monte, and Casa Del Sol; on the next terrace, the recreational improvements and finally at bottom level, the support facilities to the entire complex.

At Asilomar, located in the center of the casually circular or oval site planning arrangement of its key buildings, is an open space, and not a massive edifice as at San Simeon. The open space serves as the "commons" where guest-participants can assemble for various activities. The counterpart

centerpiece building to the "Casa Grande" in San Simeon's
scheme of things is the Phoebe Apperson Hearst Social Hall
in Asilomar's scheme of things. While the "Casa Grande"
literally dominates over all the other structures and the overall
scene, the Social Hall building's importance is gained by its
location among the key buildings and its west-facing
orientation to the Pacific Ocean in the overall plan, but not
by virtue of its size or shape or aesthetic treatment. The Social
Hall has a "leadership" role but not a dominating one in the
architectural scheme of things. These two building
arrangements, in combination with their respective
topographies, have symbolic implications. San Simeon is
arranged physically and socially in a hierarchical manner,
whereas Asilomar's physical layout is essentially on a level
plane and socially egalitarian. San Simeon evokes, for the
most part, self-indulgence, while Asilomar evokes social
solidarity. In linguistic-expressive terms, the program,
character and ambiance of San Simeon speaks to us from the
mood of the first person singular "I," and Asilomar speaks to
us from the mood of the third person plural "we." In this
respect they both reveal the differing nature of their places
and purposes, as well as the nature of the respective clients
from which they originate.

Other aspects of these two architectural complexes bear
comparison. Asilomar's site was virtually flat in contrast with
San Simeon whose steep slopes represented much greater
complexities and difficulties for siting buildings and for
construction efforts. These burdens were only added to by
Mr. Hearst who was ever requesting revisions to the
accomplished work.[8] San Simeon's steep slopes and barren
and rocky terrain required a great deal of architectural
landscape work. A network of retaining walls, walkways and
stairs as well as the massive cultivation of trees, bushes,
flowers and ground covers were developed in response to
these circumstances by Julia Morgan, whereas at Asilomar,

with the naturally existing density of trees, she had to remove only those required for each building site and for creating walking pathways and service roads to each of them, otherwise the natural landscape is left in place, uncultivated. It might be noted here, regarding site planning and landscaping, Walter Steilberg commented that Julia Morgan's strongest point of architectural design was her habit of "... working from the inside out, including the out-of-doors." "She was a landscape architect, and she knew just where the paths were to go. She was always particular about that."[9] In this connection, Julia Morgan was a great admirer of the artist-architect Charles Adams Platt, particularly his views of landscape design and its interrelationship with buildings. Later, when we take up the artistic and experiential considerations of the Asilomar buildings, we will make note of how the walking paths Julia Morgan laid out there, not only permit travel to and between the buildings, but how these "control" our experiencing them and contribute to certain impressions she wants us to have of them.

Turning now to the nature of their respective architectural characters, San Simeon's buildings are eclectically inspired by and reflective, generally, of the "Mediterranean" approach and Asilomar's buildings are inspired by and reflective of the region's "Arts and Crafts" approach; each approach was deemed "appropriate" by common consent of both clients and architect.

Unlike San Simeon, Asilomar's buildings reflect no manipulation of form or surfaces, nor the addition of ornament for stylistic effects or to create historical allusions. At Asilomar, almost all the architectural expression is derived from the natural qualities of the materials used in their structural roles or serving utilitarian purposes, in the manner of the arts and crafts goals. The employment of other decorative art forms in relation to the buildings is completely absent. Asilomar's buildings are straightforward, wooden structures. In a few cases concrete is used as a sub-strate structure with stone cladding applied; whereas, at San Simeon concrete is the main material with overt architectural expression subordinated to the stylistic terms chosen. San Simeon's architecture is conceived and developed in a Moorish-Spanish style and the overall building forms and their features and decoration are bent on delivering this image and feeling. The use of these two architectural styles is intended to engender in us two very different relationships. San Simeon's architectural character is intended to be immediately dramatically attractive and intensely interesting, exacting from us explicit reactions, while at Asilomar, the architectural character is intended to subtly serve as background where we are tacitly moved to our reactions. San Simeon's buildings are designed for stimulating active interest and visually dramatic reward, while the buildings at Asilomar are intentionally designed for easy intelligibility and casually interested observations. The overall ethos of San Simeon is an elaborate hedonism, that of Asilomar is simple modesty. The first is that of the individual client, Mr. William Randolph Hearst and the second apropos of the institutional client, the YWCA, to which their architect, Julia Morgan, serviced their expression.

Building interiors reflect these or similar observations as well. San Simeon's rooms are intensely elaborate and manipulated for visual and sensual effects, incorporating many artifactual "possessions" of the Hearst collections as well as being stage settings for their observation and appreciation. The interiors of the buildings at Asilomar are, for the most part, direct reflections of the materials used and the structural and basic architectural elements by which they are formed. There is no use made of artifacts or elaborate ornamentation of surfaces to generate their ambiance; the interiors serve as simple, comfortable, backgrounds to the social activities they house. In sum, the interior and the exterior of buildings and other cultivated architectural and landscape features of San Simeon are mainly intended to showcase the possessions of their owner, William Randolph Hearst; whereas, Asilomar's buildings and landscape is mainly intended to comfortably house a social cultural fair. Both are "retreats," but each is so in vastly different ways. Hearst Castle is conceived predominately for "exhibition" purposes, while Asilomar is conceived predominately and simply for "accommodation" purposes.

Considering the larger geographical and social context in which the two projects are located, these also differ greatly. San Simeon, located midway between Los Angeles and San Francisco, is set in the middle of a privately owned ranch, surrounded by a huge acreage of natural landscape, with the nearest major township about forty miles distant. Asilomar, on the other hand, is located within and is surrounded, for the most part, by the township of Pacific Grove, the physical environment and social existence of which had a major influence upon its establishment. The very founding and development of the cultural and commercial forces of Pacific Grove were significant factors in the YWCA Board of Trustees' opportunity and final decision to create its summer camp facility there. To the founding events and characteristics of this township we now turn.

Casa Grande, Hearst Castle, San Simeon.

Aerial View of Hearst Castle Grounds.

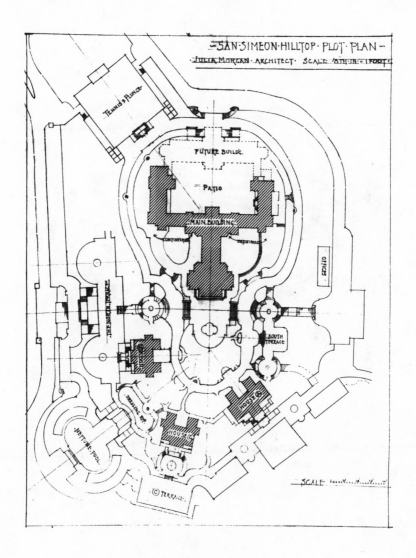

Plot Plan of Hearst Castle.

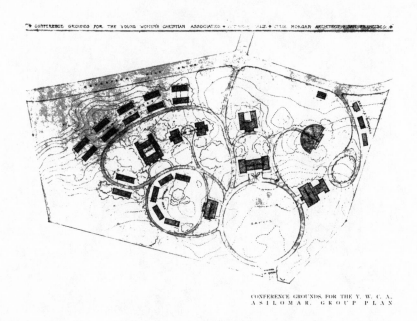

CONFERENCE GROUNDS FOR THE YOUNG WOMEN'S CHRISTIAN ASSOCIATION ♦ JULIA MORGAN ARCHITECT SAN FRANCISCO ♦

CONFERENCE GROUNDS, FOR THE Y. W. C. A.,
A S I L O M A R. G R O U P P L A N

Original Plot Plan of Asilomar—1912.

THE SITE OF ASILOMAR, PACIFIC GROVE: THE ORIGINS OF A MONTEREY BAY TOWNSHIP

The founding of Pacific Grove was unusual compared to other small towns of California. Most settlements arise out of some form of material economic need and available natural resources. However, as we will come to see, Pacific Grove's inception was for the most part, connected with religious motivations.

Located immediately to the west of the city of Monterey, Pacific Grove's borders consist of spectacular scenic ocean shoreline on its north and west edges. It has Del Monte Forest and Pebble Beach at its southern border. Until 1875 the entire area was a dense forest of pine trees. The term "grove" in its name likely arose due the removal of a major portion of tree growth on the northern shoreline by the local sawmills making lumber for building development.

The city of Monterey is one of the oldest communities in North America. For over seventy years it had served as the capital under three governments; the Spanish and the Mexican periods of Alta California and the early stages of American statehood until the Gold Rush when all major economic and political events shifted northward. The harbor of Monterey Bay had drawn international visitors and settlers from the time of its discovery, exploration and "pioneer frontier" history. The city of Monterey remained the capital and site of activities throughout the period of Anglo-American annexation. To have a township spring up and develop just adjacent to such a vital city was very unusual. Pacific Grove has a unique and intriguing history, virtually attributable to one individual.

In 1870 the population of Monterey stood at just over eleven hundred persons. Among those was David Jacks, a Scotsman, who came to America in 1847 and worked as a civilian accountant with a military unit in San Francisco. Jacks' significance lies primarily in his acquisition of lands. He came to Monterey in 1849 originally to work as a clerk in a merchant dry goods and grocery store. He arrived at the time of the closing of the Mexican War and the height of gold rush fever when Monterey's population was, for the most part, moving north to the gold fields and when much confusion reigned over land rights.

While soon after his arrival Jacks became a successful farmer, his major wealth and influence derived from his land exploits pursued in part by means of his position as the Monterey County treasurer. Jacks, observant of the tax roles, began filing on doubtful grant titles and lending money to local landowners who put up their property as collateral. Through a steady stream of foreclosures Jacks found an appetite, which quickly became a "lust," for land ownership. Eventually, by means of forfeitures, filing quit claims, rentals, leases, trades and sales, he parlayed his holdings to nearly one hundred thousand acres of land around the city of Monterey, including the future Pacific Grove area. Jacks, in one instance alone, managed to acquire thirty thousand acres of Pueblo lands of Monterey through a questionable public auction held by the city government in 1859; it came to be known, as "the rape of Monterey." From this event the habitual use by locals of the pejorative phrase "David Jacks

County" nearly replaced that of "Monterey County" as a place reference. To this day his name is attached to Jacks Peak the highest point overlooking Monterey Bay and further memorialized in a product known as "Monterey Jack" cheese, which had its beginning about 1892. Among the lands of interest for our story, which were a part of Jacks holdings were the 2,667-acre Rancho Punta de Pinos, immediately to the south, Rancho El Pescadero running from about seal rock to Carmel, both ocean coastline properties, and adjoining these, the Rancho Aquajito lands.

Along with his passion for land ownership, Jacks was moved to use some of his wealth to assist "deserving people and to promote commendable causes." He was an active churchgoer and a perennial Sunday school teacher. These activities prompted him to contribute heavily to the founding of churches. One of his undertakings was his financial and property donation to build a Presbyterian Church in Monterey. In the summer of 1873, Jacks gave permission to a Methodist minister, W. S. Ross, and his wife, both at the time in ill health, to build a small shack as a residence on his property in a fairly dense grove of pine trees located along the shoreline west of the City of Monterey near Point Pinos. The Ross's had come from the East in the interest of improvement of their health and found the wooded area suitable as well as very attractive. During the summer of 1874, a friend, Bishop J. T. Beck, a member of the Methodist Retreat Association clergy headquartered in San Francisco, spent some time visiting the Ross's. Beck had been actively meeting since 1871 with various Methodist clergy seeking a suitable location in Northern California for a summer campsite to hold church meetings. It was Ross who, in discussions, convinced the bishop that the pine forest along the seashore would be an ideal location for a summer retreat camp and suggested contacting Jacks for his assistance. David Jacks indicated his willingness to offer about one hundred acres of land and assist in the financing for the encampment to advance the adventure. The offer was in a form of a sum of money on a loan basis tied to the property as collateral.

In a meeting held on June 1, 1875, at the Howard Street Methodist Church in San Francisco, with Bishop Beck presiding, the idea of establishing a Christian Seaside Resort campground was considered and the name "Pacific Grove Retreat Association" was adopted. Negotiations were opened with David Jacks for establishing the final arrangement toward obtaining the site. Jacks provided the land and made a loan of $12,631.95 to the Association for the agreed-upon purpose of founding a retreat, not merely to hold religious meetings, but to afford a summer resort for Christian people, a place for recreation and education away from work and other distracting environments.

The plan called for a large portion of the land to be generally divided into lots thirty feet wide and sixty feet deep from street lines suitable for tenting purposes and others divided suitably to build small cottages and other facilities. The lots were to be sold on a long-term, low payment financial basis, as the project called for financial self-sustainment. About a dozen cottages and numerous tents were set up the first year to accommodate about four hundred and fifty persons. The adventure was successful in most respects, including sales and visitor attendance in its early phase; however, in a latter phase, it failed to meet its loan payments in a timely manner and the unsold property reverted back to Jacks under the terms of agreement. He decided to continue the sale of the remaining lots on his own.

In 1881, Jacks sold seven thousand acres of the Rancho El Pescadero and Rancho Punta de Pinos lands to the Pacific Improvement Company, a holding company of Southern Pacific Railroad. On March 31, 1883, Jacks reached another sales agreement with the Pacific Improvement Company for more lands, including the site of Pacific Grove, whereby the latter would retain the financial management, and the Pacific Grove Retreat Association would continue to have "moral and prudential control" over the grounds. This control would extend a distance of one mile in radius from the center of the original campsite grounds. Due to his landholdings and agricultural interests, Jacks in 1874 had financed the construction of a narrow gauge rail line from Salinas to Monterey. The line was built to move farm products in the valley to the port of Monterey for shipment by boat to various destinations. The Southern Pacific Railroad had placed track from San Francisco to San Jose in 1864, to Gilroy in April 1869, then to Salinas in September 1872 extending it to Soledad by 1873. This allowed Southern Pacific to directly compete with Jacks' line. In 1879, Southern Pacific purchased and demolished the narrow gauge Monterey-Salinas Valley Railroad connecting line and replaced it with its own broad gauge track but connected it to the then existing Watsonville terminus point in the line from San Francisco. The Southern Pacific Railroad, now having a fully developed link to the Monterey Peninsula from San Francisco, naturally had to develop reasons to attract potential passengers to use the line, since the valley route from the San Francisco Bay Area was mainly freight traffic going to Los Angeles, which was finally connected with a track by December 1900. The activities identified were the recreation, tourism and vacation markets. Southern Pacific's subsidiary holding company, the Pacific Improvement Co., first undertook in early 1880 to build the palatial Hotel Del Monte and resort facilities for fashionable clientele,[1] to the northeast of the city of Monterey. Subsequently, they decided to further the development of the Pacific Grove area as a logical place for the "religiously" inclined visitor or settler. It extended a line through Monterey to the Grove where it built a passenger station, among other facilities, and extended a spur track to

the Moss Beach area near Lake Majella, with a terminus at a
sand milling plant. This leg of track was planned to continue
to Carmel Bay but was never completed. Southern Pacific
then embarked on a promotion campaign and encouraged
thousands of San Franciscans to make a one day picnic
excursion to the seaside resort areas.

In 1884 the Pacific Improvement Co., stimulated by
increased visitor traffic, began to make addition after addition
to the original Pacific Grove lot divisioning and prices surged.
The land boom began. The retreat became a township. The
popularity of the area brought thousands of summer visitors,
and a steady increase in permanent year-round residents.
Many middle-class settlers of no particular religious
inclinations began buying land in the area outside of the
encampment and building their residences.

Purchase and resale limits to certain ethnic groups and
behavioral restrictions were incorporated into property deeds
many of which had their origin in the founding of the retreat,
and subsequently were rooted in the 1883 agreement between
the Pacific Improvement Co. and David Jacks. Land
ownership was subject to cancellation of title, if found in
violation. The laws were stringently enforced for over a
quarter of a century. At the turn of the century they became
somewhat diluted but continued to mold community conduct
in Pacific Grove as late as 1920, even then introducing deed
regulations dealing with a restrictions for such things as dancing
parties and specifying clothing for bathing. The religious
fervor began to wane after the 1920s.

Of great significance in Pacific Grove's founding and
development, and almost entirely responsible for the town's
early educational emphasis, was the Chautauqua, a late
nineteenth-century, religious adult educational institution and
cultural fair initiated by Protestant churches. The "Chautauqua"

began in 1873 when Dr. John Heyle Vincent, a Methodist minister from Plainfield, New Jersey, and Lewis Miller, a successful businessman from Akron, Ohio, visited the shores of Lake Chautaququa in southwestern New York to inspect an existing campsite-meeting ground and its facilities to determine if it would be a suitable place for the Sunday school teachers' training retreat they were planning. Apparently the name of the lake derives from metal plates placed by Captain Bienville de Celeron, in 1749, as a token of French sovereignty and bearing the name "Tchadakoin," a French spelling of a Seneca Indian tribe word. Coming upon the scene later the British pronounced the word "Chadaqua" and several variant spellings developed until 1859 when by local government decree officially change the spelling to "Chautauqua." Interpretations of the meaning of the word vary. One story has it to be a compound of two Seneca words, meaning "fish" and "take out."

The proposed summer camp was named the "Sunday School Teachers' Assembly" and was under the governance and direction of the Sunday School Association of the Methodist Episcopal Church. Dr. Vincent, the first general agent of the Sunday School Union, was a leader in the growing Sunday School Movement in the United States. The idea, based on the belief that the foundation of religious life should be laid in childhood, was to provide opportunity for teachers to meet and train and prepare for classes. Uniform standards, examinations and diplomas were part of the structure. Fairly early its program progressed toward a greater range of secular study and interest and grew into a combination of church sermons, teacher summer schools and literary and political lectures, travelogues and scientific conventions, flower shows and cooking exhibits, music concerts, plays and debates. Eventually, an offshoot created a formula that combined local, state, national and international talent, traveling from place to place on a scheduled and program basis. Notable names headed programs in such diverse subjects as biology, zoology, nature studies, history, art, sciences, cooking, travel and bible studies to name a few among the featured presentations, as well as the music concerts and dramatic plays. In 1876 the assembly officially took the name "Chautauqua" and transformed its program into a curious mix of bible evangelicalism and popular moralism, together with scientific inquiry and secular education.

Bishop Beck brought the program of the Chautauqua Assembly to Pacific Grove for its first meeting held outdoors on June 30, 1879. The next year's gathering was held in a big tent, and in 1881, a large building had been erected for the assembly. Beginning in the summer of 1887 Chautauqua picnics were convened in the area of Moss Beach and nearby Lake Majella, a favorite pleasure spot. The lake's original name was "Laguna de los Ajolotes (Lake of the Water Dogs). This lake was re-named by Mrs. George Crocker, while on a picnic there with a group of friends, "Lake Majella" meaning "Wood Dove Lake." This very site was later to be offered and chosen by the YWCA for creating the Asilomar conference and campgrounds.

Because of its popularity, Pacific Grove became nationally known as the "Chautauqua of the West." Southern Pacific promoted it to attract touring visitors, using in part its own promotional Sunset Magazine for the purpose. The Chautauqua summer forums led many participants to return, purchase property and build summer cottages. Teachers, university professors, and retiring professionals topped the list. Pacific Grove, by the turn of the century, reached about one thousand five hundred permanent residents, apart from part-time seasonal homeowners. The national popularity of the Chautauqua began to decline in the 1920s, influenced in part by the advent of radio and film medias and the

automobile. The Chautauqua's final meeting was held in
Pacific Grove on August 7, 1926.

Pacific Grove became incorporated in 1889. The final
boundaries of Pacific Grove date to the departure of the
Pacific Improvement Co. Samuel E. Morris, who had joined
the company in 1908, was charged with liquidating certain
assets toward settling the various "Big Four" family estate
interests. In doing so Morris formed the Del Monte Properties
Company, a landholding venture created out of the settlement
of the Crocker family estate. He appraised the company's
interest and decided to sell its holdings in the Pacific Grove
area to turn its full attention to the development of the more
lucrative Seventeen Mile Drive Pebble Beach and Del Monte
Forest areas located at the southern boundaries of Pacific
Grove. Morris divested the company's remaining property
interest in Pacific Grove by auctioning off its lots and by
selling, for a nominal price, various other strategic portions
of land to the city itself (for example the waterfront), which
was to be restricted from building and remain open land for
public use and interest.

It was the development of these circumstances, the
creation of Pacific Grove township and the unusual social
conditions engendered by the Chautauqua, that served as
the background circumstance by which the Pacific
Improvement Co. came to offer the site to the YWCA for the
establishment of Asilomar.

Pacific Grove, 1878
(Tent City Scene).

Pacific Grove, early 1880's
(Forest Street Scene).

THE ASILOMAR CONFERENCE GROUNDS:
THE MANNER AND COURSE OF
ITS FOUNDING

Although Julia Morgan grew up and began her career during times of increasing awareness of women's rights, she herself was not an active reformist and did not consider herself a "feminist." Women activists established their own organizations throughout the nation long before women's suffrage became an issue. In 1858 Mrs. Marshall O. Roberts organized a "Ladies Christian Association" in New York. It grew in such numbers and influence that in 1876 it was reorganized under the name of "Young Ladies Christian Association." In 1866 Mrs. Henry F. Durant founded the "Young Women's Christian Association" in Boston, the name by which we know the institution today. The YWCA had a fourfold purpose of providing temporary accommodations, recreation, instruction and social companionship for the numbers of young women who were migrating to urban cities in search of employment. By the time Julia Morgan began her architectural practice, the YWCA had become a major force in the women's movement. Having established itself in California, the YWCA had held, besides its Pacific Region National Board meetings, various summer retreat conferences on a "host" or "rental basis" at different locations, two at Mills College in 1896 and 1897, others in following years in Capitola, a township of Santa Cruz County.

The process, which culminated in the creation of Asilomar, began in March 1911, when the philanthropist Mrs. Phoebe Apperson Hearst, a longtime patron of the YWCA, contacted Miss Berth Conde, who was presiding over that year's Pacific conference meeting of the national board. Mrs. Hearst invited Miss Conde to her home in Pleasanton, California, known as "The Hacienda", and Mrs. Hearst proposed holding the 1912 summer retreat function of the Pacific Conference at The Hacienda's spacious facilities and grounds. The Hacienda del Pozo de Verona, its full name, was originally designed by the San Francisco architect A. C. Schweinfurth and built in the years 1895 to 1898. Julia Morgan had recently completed an addition and several alterations on the Hacienda for Mrs. Hearst from 1903 to 1910.

The summer retreat conferences had been regularly held in rented accommodations at Capitola. The growing success of these summer conferences had produced overcrowded conditions and Mrs. Hearst felt that the YWCA needed a permanent retreat site in California that it would own and control. Holding the next summer retreat at The Hacienda would provide a setting in which Board delegates and specially invited guests might be more easily persuaded to secure such a site and to construct suitable buildings on it. Toward this purpose, Mrs. Hearst suggested contacting the Pacific Improvement Company, which owned extensive properties in the Monterey Bay Area.

The Pacific Improvement Company, to which Mrs. Hearst referred, was a very large holding company in California, formed about 1869 by C. P. Huntington, Mark Hopkins, Leland Stanford and Charles Crocker. These men were known nationally as the "Big Four" due to their great wealth, influence and power. The company, headquartered in San Francisco, held vast tracts of land in the United States and played a significant role in the development of projects on these lands, particularly with the strategic locating of railroad services as the primary access to them. The company further underwrote the development of roadways, electricity, water and other services to support the subdividing of lots for marketing. The investment activities of the company extended as far as the Southern states and Texas, but were especially concentrated in California.[1]

Miss Harriet Taylor, executive secretary of the national board of the YWCA, in a meeting with Mrs. Hearst subsequent to the Hacienda YWCA Summer Conference, received the further suggestion that she and Miss Conde contact Harriet Alexander (Crocker) to seek their guidance in approaching the Pacific Improvement Company. Miss Conde wrote to Mrs. Alexander in March 1912 conveying Mrs. Hearst's offer and suggestions, and asked for counsel. Mrs. Alexander in turn wrote in April 1912 to Mr. Adam D. Shepard, General Manager of the Pacific Improvement Co. at his office in the Crocker Building in San Francisco. This writing served as a letter of introduction of Miss Conde to Mr. Shepard and also explained her purpose in calling upon him in the near future. Miss Harriet Taylor followed with a letter to Mr. Shepard indicating she and Miss Blanche Geary, head of the economics department of the national board, would be in San Francisco in May and asked if it would be possible to meet with him regarding the possibility of securing a permanent site for their summer conference gatherings. Mr. Shepard almost immediately returned a note indicating that he would be pleased to meet with them and that he thought there were appropriate and advantageous locations among the various properties the Pacific Improvement Company held in Monterey perhaps more than any other locality, given his understanding of their expressed purposes.

A field trip to Pacific Grove and Rancho Point Pinos areas in Monterey was undertaken to survey prospective locations.

One of the sites was 'Guardamar' (literally meaning watch-by-the-sea), part of an undeveloped wooded area at the ocean that had been already designated by the company for public use. It was often used by Methodists for their "Chautauqua Conference" programs. It was situated on the Coast in the sand hill area at Moss Beach located between Point Joe to the South and Point Pinos, with its lighthouse station, to the north. The Guardamar site was at the time only accessible by train and dirt road. The Southern Pacific railroad serviced the Monterey area from San Francisco via a railhead at Castroville to a rail yard and passenger depot at Pacific Grove, the site of a fast developing community. From Pacific Grove, a spur track was in place to a station called Majella Depot located near the Guardamar site, continuing on to terminate at a sand mining plant which produced 'Del Monte White Sand' especially processed for making green and amber glass insulators.

The Guardamar site quickly became the main focus and the favorite one during the field trip. A meeting at the nearby famous Del Monte Resort Hotel complex in Monterey owned and developed by the Pacific Improvement Co. immediately followed. The purpose of the meeting was to discuss possible terms by which a donation of property could be offered. The terms developed were mutually advantageous. From the Pacific Improvement Company's standpoint, the site was not likely to become marketable for some time. It was already allotted for public uses, and having an owner-occupant of such character would bring hundreds of visiting friends to patronize the Del Monte Resort and Pacific Grove Retreat area. It would also be an advertising feature for various properties to be made available for sale and would increase their worth many times on that account alone. In fact, the development was seen to have the potential to quadruple the property value for the company's Monterey properties estimated to be as much as ten times the donation value. The terms of offer for donation were generally set out at this meeting, although the detailed terms later varied, as did the acreage size. The YWCA was to occupy and equip the location with appropriate and permanent buildings to a value not less than $30,000 within ten years, and when so equipped could call for the property deed in full to be transferred to themselves. During the interim years the premises were to be leased at a nominal rate of $1.00 per acre, per year, the acreage to be more or less a maximum of thirty acres. The YWCA would be obligated to pay all taxes. The land was to be used exclusively for the identified purpose and for gatherings of kindred associations. If the failure to meet the terms, purposes of use, or to fully equip the site or abandonment were to occur, the title would lapse and the property would revert back to the donor. The advantages to the YWCA became obvious to its representatives in a follow up field trip to the site after this meeting.

Subsequently, during the summer conference at Mrs. Hearst's Hacienda in Pleasanton, a discussion of the Guardamar site involved some of the most prominent patrons of the YWCA, including Mrs. Ethel Crocker, Mrs. Ide Wheeler, and Mrs. Mary Merrill among others. Although some concerns had arisen about the summer dense fog and cool temperatures at a site so near the ocean, they were quickly allayed. The Pacific Improvement Company's offer was introduced to Mrs. Hearst who was favorably impressed, seeing many advantages and no disadvantages. Mrs. Hearst suggested that they disregard the other available offer of free land in Carmel[2] and arrange to accept the Pacific Improvement Company's offer, if possible, especially since they were an established company with a good reputation. The Pacific Coast territorial committee of the national board moved to accept the proposal and sent their recommendation to the national board for their final official acceptance, which was expected to occur during the October 1912 meeting in New York.

A record of a field trip to the prospective site in September 1912 reflected the mood of enthusiasm for its benefits. In the words of Mrs. Mary S. Merrill, "How well I remember that autumn afternoon and the little group of pioneer workers and dreamers who responded to the call of Mrs. Hearst and Mr. A. D. Shepard, a representative of the Pacific Improvement Company, to go to inspect the thirty acres of land offered by that company with the stipulation that we pay the taxes and put on $30,000 improvements in ten years. Mrs. Phoebe A. Hearst, Mrs. Benjamin Ide Wheeler, Miss Julia Morgan, Miss Ella Schooley, Mr. Shepard, and myself made up the personnel of this little group and together we wandered through the picturesque camping grounds of old Monterey and Pacific Grove, over the sand dunes, on thru the pine trees, gathering inspiration every moment from the glimpse of the ocean, blue in its tranquility; the scene growing more fascinating and captivating at every turn, until we reached the marvelous beach, the boundary of our possessions to be. Retracing our steps, with Miss Morgan in our lead, who visualized for us the future sites for the various buildings, we would meet the requirements of the company and recommended the National Board that this offer be accepted. Thus the vision of the Conference Grounds and Vacation Camp of the National Board became a reality."[3]

The conference center was to have the name "Asilomar." It is a conjunction of two Spanish words literally meaning, "refuge by the sea." This name was arrived at as a result of the association's open competition, the winning submission being made by Miss Helen Salisbury, a Stanford University student.

Julia Morgan was invited to participate in this September site visit because of Phoebe Hearst's recommendation or request that she be the architect for the new conference center. Mrs. Hearst not only knew Julia Morgan from the Mining and

Greek Theater projects at Berkeley, but Julia Morgan had recently been retained to accomplish remodeling work at her "hacienda" in Pleasanton, among other services. As the above quoted recollection of the autumn site tour well indicates, Julia Morgan's conceptual design of what was to become Asilomar was derived by visitations to the site and taking notice of its features. There was the gray tone of the sandy soil, the plentiful tall pines and cypress trees, the gentle sloping terrain that characterized its topography. The presence at the site of brilliant blue skies producing marked shades and shadows were shared with the oft presence of cool gray fog. These together with the warm colored ambiance of the westerly sunsets, the magnetic attraction of the Pacific Ocean, the mild even temperature, the moist sweet and salty olfactory qualities of the air, the acoustics of the southwesterly breezes rushing the trees and the ocean breakers in the distance, constituted much of the site-setting's physical and physiognomic ingredients.

The coupling of these site factors with her institutional client's programmatic purposes to establish a place for rest, relaxation, recreation and informal conference and social activities, Julia Morgan identified the style of architecture she felt appropriate. She selected the materials that would best serve to be economical and generate the structural and aesthetic results suitable to the goal of allowing several small buildings to be introduced and arranged as unobtrusively into the landscape as possible and aesthetically blend with it. The basic materials chosen were primarily Douglas fir and redwood and local riverbed stones and quarried sandstone which, left in their natural appearances, would provide the desired colors and textures to echo those of the surroundings. From this we can gain a sense of the strength of influence that the qualities of California's natural setting and climate had on shaping the character of the architecture to be designed for Asilomar. To considering these artistic qualities and Julia Morgan's design temperament we now turn.

YWCA Committee for Asilomar Leadership Conference, 1912
(Phoebe Apperson Hearst toward right wearing
silk-brocade Chinese robe).

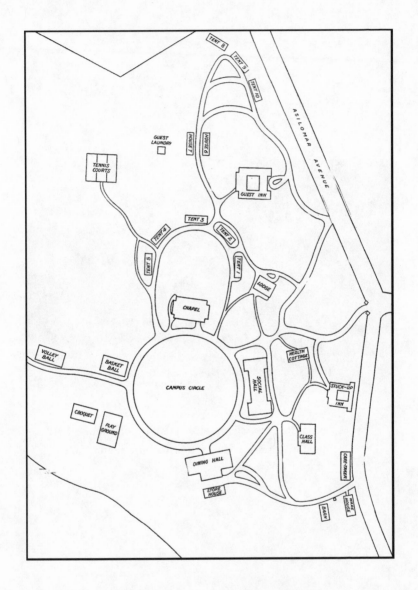

Asilomar Development Site Plan, Circa 1923.

Asilomar Train Station.

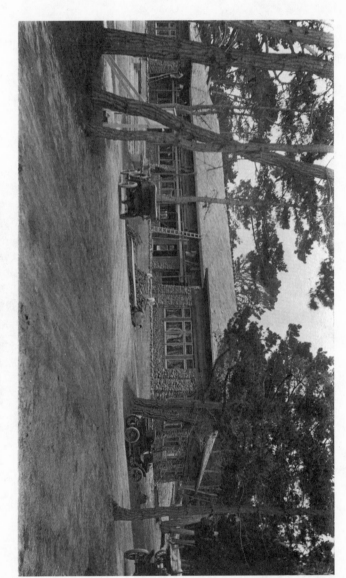

Phoebe A. Hearst Social Hall, 1912
(Building under Construction).

Phoebe A. Hearst Social Hall
(Northwest Corner View).

Phoebe A. Hearst Social Hall
(View toward Reception Desk Area).

Phoebe A. Hearst Social Hall
(View toward Library & Classroom Area).

Asilomar Tent Houses.

Mary Ann Crocker Dining Hall.

Mary Ann Crocker Dining Hall
(Main Dining Hall).

Grace H. Dodge Chapel.

Grace H. Dodge Chapel
(Southwest Corner View).

Grace H. Dodge Chapel.
(Main Hall)

Grace H. Dodge Chapel
(Altar and Window Screen).

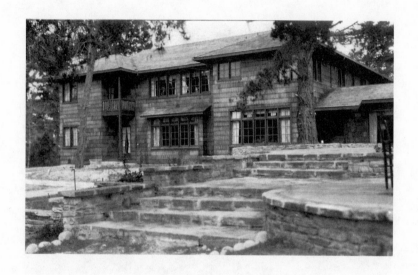

Ellen B. Scripps Lodge.

Ellen B. Scripps Lodge
(Living Room).

Stuckup Inn.

Stuckup Inn
(Living Room).

Guest Inn.

Pirates Den.

Health Cottage.

The Lodge.

The Lodge
(Living Room).

The Lodge
(Main Stair down to Living Room).

Mary S. Merrill Hall.

Mary S. Merrill Hall
(Main Hall)

Mary S. Merrill Hall
(Truss and Clerestory detail).

Mary S. Merrill Hall
(Southside)

ASILOMAR'S JULIA MORGAN BUILDINGS: ARTISTICALLY CONSIDERED

Innumerable factors come into play in giving the final shape and characteristic features to the design of buildings, ranging from the imperative and compelling to the idiosyncratic and gratuitous.

Julia Morgan was more interested in and devoted to the livability, workability and constructability of her project designs than in exploring visual drama, manipulating decorative effects or striving for cleverness or novel innovation for its own sake. Her inclination and efforts sought a sound and apt architecture, straightforward in presentation. As the architectural historian Sally Woodbridge said: "Brilliant concepts or emphasis on design as a thing in itself had little place in her work. Quality, permanence and appropriateness were paramount."[1]

A conceptual clue to this orientation, apart from the evidence of her buildings, may be found in her favored use of the nineteenth century theorist A. W. N. Pugin's saying that architecture consisted in "Commodity, Firmness and Propriety." Pugin's wording is a variant of Vitruvius's famous Latin formulation, Firmitas, Commoditas and Venustas, which in Sir Henry Wotton's English translation is "firmness, commodity and delight." The term venustras or "delight", in the original formulation is replaced by Pugin with "propriety" as a basic value category. "Delight," historically, stood for what was considered from the times of antiquity to be the ultimate aim of architecture, namely beauty. The substitution of "propriety" in the formulation permitted a free eclecticism rather than the strict imitation of past architectural styles required of revivalism. The notion that one style is best for all occasions is replaced by the choosing of one style, or a combination of styles, for each individual occasion.

However the meaning of "propriety" in this context is restricted in its significance to aesthetics, whereas its connotations in the context of the Arts and Crafts Movement sensibilities and concerns was much wider, having to do with social as well as artistic matters. Here, it carried a sense of obligation, which is to say that "propriety" is accorded certain sovereignty as an approach to the making or the having of things.

Julia Morgan's professional concern was to deliver eclectically appropriate buildings to her clients and provide historically founded architectural continuity to society. Evidence for this is Julia Morgan's extensive library of architectural monographs and folios, which she, throughout her career, consulted along with her clients at the very outset of a commission to determine an appropriate approach from which to develop the project.

How a work of architecture comes to be what it is often greatly constrained by individual clients as for example we have seen in the case of William Randolph Hearst and his influence on the design of "Hearst Castle" at San Simeon illustrates. But even this example can appear modest when contrasted with another rather extreme kind of client mandate that Julia Morgan announced one day to her office staff. Placing on the drawing board photographs given to her by a new client, she commented: "Well, we have something new here. We have a front of a house and we have to put a back on . . . he wants a house that looks like this, and he wants all those things put in back of it."[2]

Having been chosen to be the architect for Asilomar, Julia Morgan was apparently entrusted with a free hand in the design of the various buildings for Asilomar, constrained only by her clients brief consisting of the stated use assignment of each building and a stipulated budget limit. This is evidenced by a note that Julia Morgan sent to her secretary, Lillian Forney, in 1929. She remarked in the letter: "I [usually] design and build to please the client and their expectations. At Asilomar, the YWCA permitted me to landscape the buildings as I saw fit."

At the time of Asilomar's design, many Bay Area architects practicing under the influence of the Arts and Crafts Movement, of which Julia Morgan was one, placed strong emphasis on expressing the unique conditions peculiar to each individual project. In this approach, factors such as personal client needs, features of the building site, virtues of climate, recourse to local material sources and construction methods have a pronounced effect on the resultant form and character of the design outcome. Formal aspects, inclusions of historical motifs and association factors of a design are accorded greater or lesser latitude according to the individual architect's predilections established by academic training and personal experiences.

The ideas of the Arts and Crafts Movement exerted a considerable influence in the case of Asilomar's building designs. This is to be seen in the simplicity of the buildings, in the materials selected, formal features, color, scale and treatment of structural systems. However, the architectonic principles of academic eclecticism Julia Morgan learned at the Ecole des Beaux-Arts play a major role as well. While the influence of academic eclecticism is less obvious, it is nevertheless a significant factor. It mainly affects space planning and the compositional treatment of elements and features of the buildings. The internal space organizations are bi-axially ordered and symmetrically arranged generating the overall outward shape and mass of a building. Doors, window fenestration and other features are also arranged in symmetrical alignments axially balancing each of the facades.

Julia Morgan's approach to site planning for multiple building complexes were generally to array the buildings around a circle or oval scheme.[3] Although the individual buildings were of symmetrical design, they were arranged in a nonaxial manner or otherwise off center or line, contrary to the standard Ecole des Beaux-Arts approach. The individual buildings were sited in consideration of functional interrelationships, views, sunlight and other orientation factors. She favored this pattern of siting major buildings around a grass or garden circle or oval to perceptually establish the functional relationships between them and at the same time to enhance their relation to natural elements of the landscape. In the case of Asilomar the circle or oval served as the group assembly area, as well as being the symbolic center and marker for orientation and way finding. The pathways are designed in a manner to avert approaching any building axially head on. One approaches at an angle, usually toward one corner of the building, such that the symmetrical design of the facades is not noticed and a certain informality is obtained.

Julia Morgan seems to have recognized that building designs of simplicity, order and restraint, for achieving rustic and reposeful qualities could be obtained from combining academic classicism and the Arts and Crafts approaches. Whatever the differences and strains between these two orientations, they were not felt to be disparate but could be mutually and usefully integrated for rich and harmonious results. Julia Morgan offsets and subtly subdues the formal aspects of the buildings organization by creating textural interest, color richness and shadow variation through juxtaposing varied materials and shapes in the wall planes, giving a greater impression of informality and casual appearance than they actually have. She achieves a balanced composition of the whole while sustaining clarity in articulation of all elements and features including joints and transitions. To achieve her goal that the building's outward appearance be as unobtrusive as possible and blend into the natural landscape, local materials were selected. Riverbed granite rock, quarried sandstone, redwood, cedar, Douglas fir and oak materials are left unpainted and in their natural state of appearance all having matte finished surfaces. They are used for their inherent natural colors and textures in a straightforward manner. The scale and proportioning of the buildings are accentuated toward the horizontal, giving a look and feel of casual, comfortable repose that is appropriate for a place intended to be a casual retreat. The generously sloped roof shapes with large overhangs convey a strong sense of shelter. The use of porches patios, balconies and trellis devices offer a sense of indoors and outdoors connection and also provides relief from having overly flat-walled elevations. Construction elements are left visible for both their visual interest and display of craftsmanship. Ornamentation is kept to a subtle minimum, unadorned materials in their natural qualities being the preferred emphasis.

For Julia Morgan, the manner by which a building is constructed is as important a concern as the aesthetic appearance and spatial accommodations. The respect for technical considerations early acquired by attending the College of Civil Engineering at the University of California in Berkeley, nurtured a sensitivity not only to the construction techniques, but also the positive prospects this factor can have on a building's expressive character. Julia Morgan viewed architecture as a craft. She is well known for her avid interest in the nature of materials, both in their performance and sensible qualities, the skills of artisans, her ardent control of events at the job site and her desire to allow these factors to have an aesthetic role in determining the appearance of buildings. For example, how things are made, joined or supported are often left exposed, particularly when interior spaces are large enough to accommodate such a display of elements such as structural beams and framing or truss systems.

The goal of simplicity in this architecture does not mean the absence of ornament or the avoidance of complexity, in any reductive sense. It is concerned to allow cognitive understanding of the architecture as a coherent and all-embracing whole through a ready reading of all its parts. Simplicity is used "critically" to connote the restrained and refined character of a work in contrast to the theatrical elaborations and profusions of ornamental features.

The affective values of architecture are a power to evoke associations and mood. As it is to be a place for retreat, there is a striving to establish an appropriate mood of ease, contentment, quiet, refinement, generousness and casualness. The manner of achieving this, specifically in the Hearst Social Hall, Crocker Dining Hall, Dodge Chapel, and Lodge buildings, is the look and feel derived from the alpine mountain cabin and lodge vernacular whose affective qualities are characterized as rustic, primitive, wedded to nature, modest, simple and relaxed.

The formal style of the Ecole's "academic classicism," with its symmetrical-axial compositional principles, governs the buildings of Asilomar, but at the same time Julia Morgan avoids the assertive monumentalism and the elaborate decorativeness of civic buildings. The "freestyle" of the

English Arts and Crafts Movement, with its irregular, asymmetrical organization and its inclination toward dramatic picturesqueness and Victorian decoration, is also avoided. We find in the appearance and feeling of many of Asilomar's buildings a close connection with the wood building traditions of Northern Europe blended with regionally developed alpine idioms and to a lesser extent those of the Mediterranean and Oriental traditions.

It is assuredly remarkable testimony to Julia Morgan that these economically and aesthetically modest edifices of Asilomar, after seventy-five to over eighty-five years of existence, continue to sustain and accommodate intense use, remain physically sound, steadfastly evoke a mood of pleasantness and ease, and elicit such wide and warm admiration. These buildings and their setting, as the well-known novelist Iris Murdoch once said of her novels, are meant, "to be grasped by enjoyment." To the experiences of Julia Morgan's Asilomar buildings we now turn.

Phoebe A. Hearst Social Hall.

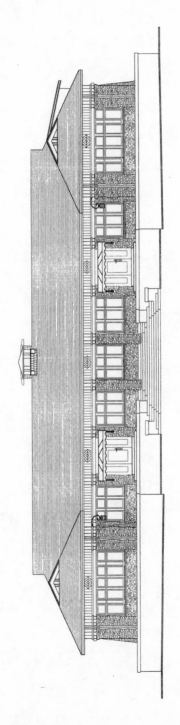

Phoebe A. Hearst Social Hall
(West Elevation).

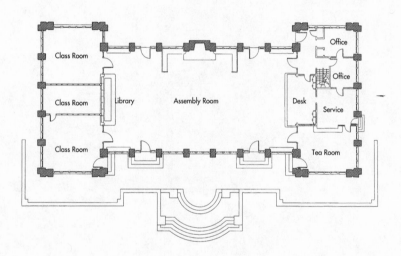

Phoebe A. Hearst Social Hall
(Floor Plan).

The Lodge.

Mary S. Merill Hall.

Stuckup Inn
(Interior court).

Stuckup Inn
(Corner detail)

ASILOMAR'S JULIA MORGAN BUILDINGS: EXPERIENTIALLY CONSIDERED

There are eleven remaining Julia Morgan buildings at Asilomar. All of these, along with the stone pillar markers forming the entrance gate, have been placed on the Registry of National Landmarks for protection. Each of these buildings has its own unique feeling in spite of the fact that they collectively are of one characteristic style. Julia Morgan sought to develop "a feeling" as the essential motif of a building. She believed that buildings could have a feeling about them that constituted their personality; their animation. It was expected that the feeling of a building would resonate in the experiences people would have in coming into contact with it. Julia Morgan's aspiration for "feeling" in buildings, which was to be imaginatively found during the design process, seems to have been inspired by Bernard Maybeck, to whom she often looked for insight in this respect. While in her office reviewing drawings with staff members, she often would remark, "See if you can't get a little more of the feeling of Mr. Maybeck," indicating that the sought-after "feeling" was the goal of aesthetic qualities generated in planning, primarily in the organization and imaging of interior space,

This conviction appears to be the basis for Julia Morgan's suspicion and impatience with those who would write or talk about architecture. She said that "buildings should speak for themselves," meaning that they must be directly visited and appreciated as you would if you genuinely wanted to know some person, or know some institution. You can only finally find them by coming into personal direct contact with them in their physical embodiments, not vicariously through verbal or written means.

In her manner of designing from the inside outward, the connection between the interior and the landscape was of great interest to Julia Morgan. In this respect she may have been greatly influenced by the artist-architect Charles Platt, whose work she especially admired for his sensitivity and the relational solutions he offered in his building designs to the landscape. At Asilomar the various structures are sited and arranged with consideration not only for orientation to sunlight and views, but also for their functional relationships. In arranging buildings at Asilomar, Julia Morgan actively looked after the logistical needs as well as the social and environmental implications. The sleeping tents and guest lodgings, as well as the Director's Cottage, are arrayed to the north of the site away from the "Commons" assembly area and its nexus of Hearst Social Hall, Dodge Chapel and Crocker Dining Hall buildings. The male and female staff lodgings, i.e., Stuck-up Inn and Pirate's Den, are located, with appropriately discrete distances between them, so as to be near Hearst Social Hall, Merrill Hall and Crocker Dining Hall. From the standpoint of food servicing, Crocker Dining Hall's kitchen service is appropriately proximate to Merrill Hall, Hearst Social Hall and Dodge Chapel, all of which have occasion to be serviced with refreshments delivered from the kitchen, as well as the considerations of the large numbers of guests having to circulate to the dining facility between formal meetings and events. Recreational facilities, such as the pool, baseball field, etc., were located in the northwest area. Julia Morgan's approach to the natural landscape topography was to essentially leave it "as is." She sited buildings on the existing soil without manipulation of terrain. As a consequence there is a subtle difference in site elevation between the Chapel, Hearst Social Hall and Dodge Dining Hall, the chapel being the highest and the dining hall the lowest as they are arrayed around the "commons" circle. While this difference affects our experience of looking at each of these buildings from the others or as we walk to one from the other, it does not evoke any sense of hierarchical relationship of importance.

Of the original sixteen structures Julia Morgan designed for Asilomar, eleven remain in use by registered guests. Eight of them hold some special experiential interests to be commented upon. The sequence of commentary follows the chronological order in which they were completed. The names given in parentheses are the names by which the structures are currently known and identified by signage.

The entry to Asilomar is marked by two stone pillars, capped by light fixtures housed in metal. Mounted on each pillar was a metal plaque originally embossed with the identifying letters YWCA. These plaques were later changed to read ASILOMAR, likely prior to 1936 when the YWCA first gave consideration to dispose of the grounds.

The road from this entry point curls its way down a slope leading directly to the strategically located Phoebe Apperson Hearst Social Hall (Administration Building) the centerpiece of Julia Morgan's vision for Asilomar's overall site plan and the first facility to be constructed. The structure was completed in 1913, to serve a number of immediate needs. The building originally was conceived to accommodate reception, administrative, social, chapel, library and classroom functions. The role and importance of this building is signaled more by its central location at the circular "commons" area in the overall plan of the grounds, and its west facing view to the Pacific Ocean, than by its size, shape or appearance, which are very similar to those of buildings nearby.

Before considering some of the architectural features of this particular building it would be well to take note of several significant modifications that have occurred which detract from the look and feel of Julia Morgan's original conception. The original stone and concrete terrace and stairs that descended gradually toward the ocean on the west side of the building have been removed and replaced with a large wood deck. Consequently the building's relationship to the terrain has shifted in appearance and feeling from being constructed "on and with" the natural slope to being "above and apart" from the site. Another site relationship modification occurred on the east side where the natural terrain was excavated back away from the building to construct the current automobile entry road and thus shifted the major entry to the east side of the building. This side of the building had originally been served only by a safety and service access path. An exterior stairway existed down to a basement area, which housed a heater room and a fireplace ash clean out chamber.

Additional modifications to the exterior of the building to be noted include the removal of all original iron lanterns, and the removal of all bark from the half log decorative frieze feature that extends around the building, including the diamond patterns that were inlaid into this frieze ribbon.

Modifications to the interior space include removal of the original wood reception counter at the south wall, the removal of the library woodwork at the north wall, the replacement of the original light chandeliers, the introduction of office partitioning that intrudes into the space at the southwest corner, the removal of the wood built-in inglenook seating at the fireplace and under the windows, and the conversion of the original classrooms located at the North end into a store and toilet facilities.

Supporting some of the general observations made earlier about Julia Morgan's active use of modern materials and techniques, it may be noted that the foundations and the exterior perimeter walls and pylons consists of poured-in-place concrete. All the exterior wall and pylon surface materials of the four facades are decorative: the river rock is veneered to the concrete structural walls and pylons, the ribbon frieze of half logs and the wood features that make up the "capitals" of each of the stone covered pylons are applied and fastened to the concrete substrate frame of the building.

There is no overt direct expression of the structural nature of the building to be found on the exterior. The only suggestion of the structural order of the design on the exterior is the regularity of the window bay system reflected by the spacing of the river rock covered pylons which support the roof structural trusses, between which the windows and doors are located. The slightly battered (sloped) stone pylons provide a subtle softening of the vertical angularity and accentuate the appearance of the roof sheltering overhangs. The interior structural king trusses, held together by decoratively shaped metal plate fasteners are entirely left exposed, as are the roof joists and rafters above these trusses, for aesthetic interest in their own right and to create the high ceiling. These two factors along with the use of unpainted natural redwood materials, the large window bays and the large fireplace make up the main aesthetic features of the interior space. The stone fireplace, with built-in inglenook seats to either side, center in the long wall opposite to the outlook to the Pacific Ocean, greatly contributed to the feeling of warmth and comfort of the hall. At the north end of the hall was the library desk with exposed book shelving behind it. To either side of this desk were doorways leading to meeting or classrooms. At the opposite end of the hall was the reception desk counter. The administrative offices were located to the east side of this counter, including a stairway to office space on a second level "attic" area. On the west side of the counter was a doorway leading to tearoom and dispensary room. These rooms likely served to provide refreshments for events held in the hall as well.

The alpine character of the exterior is accomplished by an eclectic application of materials to a technically modern concrete structural frame, while the interior character is a straightforward result of structural and functional needs refined by aesthetic interests. The "service call" bell tower housing was originally located on the roof of the Social hall and was relocated to the chapel when it was constructed.

The Grace H. Dodge Chapel completed in 1915, was located on the north side of the "commons" circle and was designed to serve multiple uses. These included lectures, religious services, classroom, theatre and social functions as well as exhibitions. Originally there was a photo development darkroom in the basement at the west end of the building for the print production of group photographs. While the south face of the chapel is symmetrical in composition with two entrances, Julia Morgan guides our approach along a pathway leading from the commons circle to the southeast corner of the building where the main entry porch to the Chapel is located. A slightly sloping floor increases visibility for the audience in the main space, and a "choir" loft is accessed by a narrow steep stair adjacent to the main entrance. Julia Morgan employed the use of large folding wood partitions to either side and to the rear of the main seating area to allow for the versatility of closing off individual spaces for a variety of simultaneous uses, or left open, for greater capacity in a fuller assembly of people. With doors in the open position a great deal of daylight is allowed to enter. When in the closed position the space can be darkened to show films for example. The north and south facing long walls of the chapel are graced with plenty of large windows, and the west wall has a large "picture" window with a direct view to the sand dunes and the Pacific Ocean. It is of some interest that the original design plans for the chapel shows an intent to have the west facing window subdivided into fairly small panes of glass, rather than the large sheets of glass presently existing. The overall interest of the interior is achieved by the careful design and modulation of the redwood panel work, the exposed structural truss work and the incorporation of large amounts of window opening, allowing penetration of light to what would otherwise be a fairly dark space in the daytime. All these devices are classic Bay Area Arts and Crafts approaches to design expressing their attractiveness in the most simple and natural terms.

The Crocker Dining Hall, completed in 1918, was designed to serve over 250 persons at one sitting. The exterior echo's the materials and many features of the Hearst Social Hall and the Dodge Chapel. The dining hall building is unique in that it is the only facility at Asilomar where there is a single entry located at the central axis of the facade. All the other buildings, including the Lodge, Scripps, Hearst Hall, Chapel and Merrill Hall, have dual main entries and all of these have their entries on minor axes of their facades. Julia Morgan, in expectation of the inevitable delay endemic to group food service, introduced a porch to provide a covered place where people can meet and pause before entering and being seated. The dormers and vents provide additional features to the roofline. The interior's large space is made even more gracious by its height, and by leaving the structural trusses exposed, the roof is effectively the ceiling of the room as well. The two large fireplaces, located symmetrically at either end of the room, provided heating. The generous amounts of window in the walls and roof dormers above the trusses maximize and balance the spread of day lighting throughout the space. The structural walls and the fireplaces are poured-in-place concrete finished with stone cladding.

The fireplaces have specially designed ceramic tile inlay features that convey Arts and Crafts sensibilities. Julia Morgan's reputation for her tile designs was considerable during her career, and ceramic tiles were a feature in many of her buildings.

It should be noted here again that the interior has been modified to the detriment of the feeling of the space. The floor level has been raised to accommodate the installation of a new heating system, which greatly reduces the height of the space and affects the overall volume.

The Lodge building, completed in 1918, was designed to accommodate visiting YWCA executives and staff. Consequently, this facility offers a few special refining features. Julia Morgan designed a two-story structure for the purpose, allowing her to develop a small but delightful redwood-paneled entry foyer-lobby featuring an enticingly simple stairway leading to an open gallery space. That space provides access to the two upper level wings of guest quarters to either side, totaling eighteen rooms in all. The Lodge is sited on a knoll just north of the Hearst Social Hall, and adjacent to the main pathway leading to the other guest sleeping facilities, including the tent houses. Julia Morgan designed the main face of the building with complete formal symmetry but established walking pathways such that one must approach the building, asymmetrically, toward its corners. Each doorway has a covered entry that supports small outside balconies above. Second-floor balconies relieve the otherwise flat exterior walls on the west and east sides of the building and provide an additional amenity for the guest rooms. The foyer-lobby has a stone fireplace and casual seating area. These, together with the large south facing windows and an overlook to the Hearst Social Hall and commons area, afford a very pleasant restful place.

Stuck-up Inn was built in 1918 to house female service staff. The staff consisted of college students who found their assigned tasks to be entirely below their station. They were labeled as being "stuck-up," and the name Stuck-up Inn became commemoratively attached to this lodging facility. Julia Morgan designed this building symmetrically about a central axis forming a U-shaped plan. Later, an addition at the east end closed the "U" converting the building to a rectangle shaped plan with a fully enclosed courtyard within. There are entry ways at either end of the living room, which faces westward for the view toward the Pacific Ocean. The brick fireplace (the only use of brick at Asilomar) is centrally located on the east wall of the room. Two doors on either side of the living room lead to wings of sleeping rooms. The corridors overlook the court. The window design of the long corridors creates a feeling reminiscent of Japanese architecture. The long horizontal and continuous strip fenestration on each side of the court is sectioned into relatively small square panes of glass, giving the impression of a screen. Julia Morgan left the living room roof support system exposed, forming debarked wood logs into a structural truss framework with a rusticity that appears almost unsystematic, even random. In the living room Julia Morgan provided built-in window alcove seating at the west wall facing the Pacific Ocean for leisure lounging. The exterior wood shingle wall cladding is softened by the larger sheltering roof overhangs and the exposed ends of round log roof rafters, a detail to be found on the sleeping tents as well as at the roofing structure of the Pirates' Den.

The Pirates' Den was completed in 1923 originally to house male staff. It was sited away from guest lodgings, on the service road near the dining hall. The term Pirates' Den came to be affixed to this building due to the habitual prank carried out each summer by the hired college student male staff, of dressing up as Pirates, including the likes of Captain

Kidd, and unexpectedly bursting into Crocker Dining Hall through the windows during dinner to considerable startling effect. Here, as in the building for female staff, Stuck-up Inn, debarked logs were used to form structural trusses supporting the roof in the small living room. Julia Morgan used this device as a means to increase the ceiling height and add visual interest to small spaces without resorting to extra expense. This use of debarked natural logs is reminiscent of that first employed in the sanctuary of the Unitarian Church of the New Jerusalem, built in San Francisco in 1894. Julia Morgan was known to have greatly admired this church. The church designed by A. Page Brown for Rev. Joseph Worcester inaugurated an approach to design that would become known as the San Francisco Bay regional form of architectural arts and crafts.

Scripps Lodge Annex (Scripps) was erected in 1927. Containing twenty-three rooms, it is like the lodge, a two-story structure symmetrically designed about a main axis in plan and exterior elevations. As an annex, it is sited immediately adjacent to the north of the Lodge building. Its entry door again is favored by the design of the walking path approach toward the corner of the building and like the Lodge has a balcony located over it. Upon entering, however, one finds oneself in a corridor where immediately to the right is a set of folding wood framed glass doors which serve the building's living room. The living room is entirely paneled with redwood board and batten material with a large stone fireplace on the north and a full set of widows facing south. Julia Morgan introduces, scale and rhythmic qualities into the interiors by the careful layout of the vertical and horizontal batts on the walls and ceilings and by altering the sizes of the vertical struts in the stair corridor hand railings. She also pays attention to the tactile qualities of the top rails and newel posts by smoothing away all sharp edges. The introduction of curved brackets at doors and windows softens the right-angled "butting" lines, offering a gentleness to the otherwise rectilinear fashion by which the elements of the building come together. The meeting room to the east side of the living room was a later addition to the facility designed by Julia Morgan.

Merrill Hall, constructed in 1928 as a large assembly hall, is conceptually reminiscent of Julia Morgan's well-known and admired St. John's Presbyterian Church in Berkeley, California, built in 1910. Despite being different in purpose, both rely on exposure of all structural material systems of their walls and roof for establishing the interior character and aesthetic effects. Both utilize the classical "basilica"[1] clearstory space design for natural lighting to the interior. Both are the result of respecting the extremely sparse budget constraints while seeking the maximum of rich and favorable experiential qualities. Both buildings consist of what Walter Steilberg, speaking of St. John's, simply called "just straight structure, wooden structure."[2] A key difference, however, between St. John's and Merrill Hall is in the wood framing. In Merrill Hall, Julia Morgan introduces curvatures in the truss members and in the wall framing, which are reflected on the exterior of the building as well. Since the interior space of Merrill Hall is much larger than St. John's Church, with its capacity to seat nearly eight hundred persons, it is likely that she felt a need, as she said in connection with solving a problem on another project, " . . . I wanted to introduce some curved lines in this building." She reasoned: "You'll find that it always helps to have some curved lines, not everything going this way and that."[3] Julia Morgan appealed to the use of local sandstone for the exterior walls in Merrill Hall to create a strong visual relationship with the ground. Since the building is a rather large volume perched on a knoll overlooking the Phoebe Hearst Social Hall and the Crocker Dining Hall, this approach helped to reduce the prospect for perceiving it as overwhelming.

Perhaps no greater tribute to the uplifting success of the experiential rewards to be garnered from the various buildings of Asilomar as designed by their architect, Julia Morgan, in complementary combination with the beauty of the natural landscape of the site, than the collective sentiments expressed by the "Stuck-ups" themselves in 1928:

"We have learned this summer together to appreciate the full meaning of Asilomar. We have grown to love it and understand the feeling that is held by people all over the World as they remember the happy days they spent here."

Summer Guests Arriving at
Asilomar Train Depot.

Arriving by transfer vehicle at
Phoebe A. Hearst Social Hall.

Festive Dinner in
Mary A. Crocker Dining Hall.

Concluding Remarks

As we have seen by virtue of our story, Julia Morgan was an exceptional person and an exceptional architect. She was unwaveringly her own person and dedicated to her chosen form of art, in all of its practical and aesthetic capacities. In practical terms Julia Morgan's buildings were to accommodate what we need or, alternatively, what we would like to do, and be structurally sound. In so many ways, while always attentive to formal qualities of design, she treated the design of buildings in their expressive capacity as metaphors, reflective of human character, revealing of what we are or, alternatively, would wish to be.

In her architecture, Julia Morgan delivered, in a pluralistic fashion, individual 'personalities' to each of her buildings, and did so in the interest of cultivating the best possible practical and aesthetic character and characteristics to each that opportunity would allow and abilities afford. On behalf of this aim, her key methodological tool was the device of 'composition'.[1] In the composing of a building's form, Julia Morgan consistently sought out a flexible balance, variously combining rigorous symmetry and casual asymmetry, in arraying features generative of architectural character. She strenuously avoided including features in her buildings that got along ill together or would otherwise detract from being an intelligible and serviceable whole. In her work, there is always not only an organized, but a harmonious feeling, the quality suggested by her frequent calling for "more of the

Maybeck feeling", not only in terms of the building edifices themselves but in relation to the landscape in which they were located. These compositional aspects are exemplified, despite their obviously unique individuality, at Hearst Castle and Asilomar, two of Julia Morgan's masterpieces.

However, as Allan Temko wrote: "Of these modest, rational buildings in wood and stone, so chaste compared to the flamboyance of her work for Hearst, none had more warmth, strength and sure feeling for the land than Asilomar, the YWCA Conference Center beside the sea at Pacific Grove".[2]

In her person, Julia Morgan may have become, in the course of her long career financially, "a woman of means". Overriding this, however, throughout she was a steadfast woman of certain 'appropriate ends' to be met. Given her prolific career, her success in that career, and the heritage she has left to us, Julia Morgan, manifestly and memorably, achieved being "a woman of accomplishment".

Appendix A

Alta California:
From Spanish Territory to
the Gold Rush and Statehood

Two major antecedent events combine in significance contributing to Julia Morgan's parents having migrated west to San Francisco, where Julia Morgan was born and raised, and to the creation of the Asilomar Conference Grounds. These consist in the historic annexation of California by the United States and especially the discovery of gold in the years 1848-49. Both occurring just twenty-three years prior to Julia Morgan's birth.

The familiar place names of California, San Francisco, Monterey and Carmel come to us from the discovery, exploration and colonization brought about with the Spanish expeditionary voyages in the Pacific Ocean by the explorers Cortez, Anza, Ulloa, Cabrillo, Drake, Vizcaino and Portola.[1] California's name is credited to Hernando Cortez from his Pacific Coast explorations dating from 1527 to 1539, which, by the 1540s, had come to be used to refer initially to what is now known as Baja California and subsequently to the western shore region of central and North America. The name was apparently derived from a widely read fifteenth-century

Spanish novel, published in Seville in 1510, entitled Las Sergas de Esplandian (The explorations of Esplandian) by Garaci Ordonez de Montalva. Cortez is believed to have had a copy of this novel in his ship's library. The word "california" appears in the novel, which describes an idyllic mythical island inhabited by Amazons, ruled by a pagan queen "Calafia," and where gold and other precious metals and stones could be plentifully found.

In 1542, Spain's Viceroy Antonio de Mendoza formed an exploration venture consisting of three ships commanded by Juan Rodriguez Cabrillo in search of the "Strait of Anian" believed to be an existing passage connecting the Pacific and the Atlantic oceans. Cabrillo explored the coast as far north as what is today known as Oregon and while doing so claimed the harbors later to be named "San Diego" and "Monterey" for Spain. Sebastian Vizcaino sailing into the Pacific coastal bay for the first time on December 16, 1602, named Monterey and the nearby inlet of Carmel. Vizcaino had been commissioned to map the California coast and search for safe harbors. He bestowed the name "Monterey" in honor of his patron in Mexico City, the Conde de Monterey, viceroy of New Spain. Vizcaino also explored the beach area and river outlet immediately to the south of the bay and named the river "El Rio Carmelo" in honor of his chaplains, who were Carmelite Fathers.

The name Carmel or Carmelite derives from a thirteenth century group of hermits who founded a monastic order called "The Order of Our Lady of Mount Carmel," thought to be a reference to the site of Mount Carmel near Jerusalem. Some years later Don Gaspar de Portola, exploring by land, first viewed the panoramic bay that was to become San Francisco, on October 11, 1769. Juan Bautista de Anza founded the Presidio San Francisco de Assisi on September 17, 1776, and Frey Junipero Serra formally dedicated the mission on October

9, 1776. On June 3, 1770, Portola and Serra returned to
Monterey for the purposes of establishing a presidio and
mission there. The mission came to be located in Carmel for
greater convenience to natural resources and was used as
Serra's headquarters for overseeing the twenty-one missions
he eventually established by the time of Mexico's gaining
independence from Spain in 1821,

By 1769 Spain claimed the lands not only of South America
and New Spain, but in the northern territory, that from the
Mississippi River westward to the Pacific coast including Baja
and Alta California. Alta California under Spanish rule, 1769
to 1821, would become, through its colonizing efforts, a land
of presidios, missions, civil pueblos and ranchos, the major
institutions created in this period.

The late eighteenth century and the early nineteenth
century saw the development of a major economic link
connecting New England with California and an active
interest by the United States governing administrations in
the annexation and settlement of the West. These were the
two most influential American forces in bringing about
California's development.

In the same year (1776) that San Francisco's presidio and
missions were being founded by the Spanish, Captain James
Cook left Plymouth Harbor, England, and after exploring the
South Pacific Islands, proceeded to the exploration of the
Alta California and Northwest coast line. Here Cook found
available, among other things, pelts from various animals such
as wolves foxes, bears, deer and particularly that of sea otters.
The sea otter pelts were regarded to be "softer and finer"
than that of any others known at the time. When Captain
Cook's expedition reached China, it was immediately realized
how valuable an article of commerce the furs were to the
market demands that existed there. John Ledyard, who served

with Cook, returned to New England where he attempted to create a similar trading venture but failed. However, Ledyard's idea survived in the efforts of William Shaws, an established merchant, who in 1784 undertook to develop international commerce for Boston by opening up trade with China, sending his merchant vessel Empress of China to Macao, then the official port of entry for Canton. This was to be followed by Joseph Barrell who conceived the idea of including the northwest into an outright "three way" trading operation. In 1787 Shaws, taking up this idea as well, sent the merchant vessels Columbia and Lady Washington to the Pacific to develop the valuable fur trade for which Canton was now the chief world market. Both of these ventures proved to be highly successful. In 1808 Captain William Shaler began publishing in a widely read magazine accounts of his lucrative voyages from the ship Lelia Byrd, including reporting in detail on the conditions and opportunities available in Alta California. By 1823 the Boston merchant company Bryant & Sturgis came to dominate almost all of California maritime trade, including competitors from foreign nations.

The significance of these "merchant adventures" lay in stimulating considerable American interest in the protected harbors of the Pacific coastline and the knowledge of natural resources of California and Oregon lands. The fur and whale shipping commerce that developed was eventually supplanted by the hide and tallow trade based on California's cattle raising ranchos introduced from Mexico, which was almost the sole land industry of the region in the 1800s. The earlier Mexican expeditions to California such as those undertaken by Rivera, Anza, Garces and Fages brought with them breeding stock cattle in considerable numbers and for which the natural conditions of California were so thoroughly congenial.

The Boston Ships, as they come to be called, traveled from New England via Cape Horn to California. A trip's duration varied from four to six months. These ships usually put in first at the port of Monterey where the only customs house was located. Trading vessels were required to do so for payment of duty fees on their cargo. Monterey had also served during most of the Mexican period as the seat of civil and military life, as well as social center of the province. The years 1841 to 1845 saw the peak presence of vessels at any one time along the coastline. Mostly by means of the hideand- tallow trade, New England began its economic and cultural commerce expansion to the Pacific coast. These were the years that novels, journals, magazines and other publications gave accounts of western scenes and experiences. This would include, for example, Thomas Farnham's Life and Adventures in California and Richard Henry Dana Jr.'s Two Years Before the Mast. The later work, published in Boston in 1840, contributed in inspiring American popular and government interest in the commercial and living habitat potential of the west. One of the few earlier publications of significance and influence was that by Captain George Vancouver, which gave extensive descriptions of California, including his ports of call at San Francisco and Monterey, from his 1792-1794 voyages with the British war vessel Discovery.

In the year 1810 Miguel Hidalgo, a rebellious priest, inaugurated the struggle for Mexican independence from Spain. Independence was achieved in 1821, including United States official recognition, and by 1822 Spanish rule ended in California. With the advent of Mexican independence, Monterey altered its view, now favoring maritime trade. At the time the Spanish population in Alta California stood at just over 3,200 many of whom were military. From the middle of the 1820s to the Mexican War in 1846, Alta California saw a considerable increase in American merchant traders. The ports commonly selected were Monterey and San Francisco the best protected and established with facilities. The hide and tallow trade derived from cattle raising, sea otter hunting along the coast and some beaver trapping in the interior continued to be the chief occupations of the province. By 1840 the Old Spanish institutions of Mexico were about to be supplanted by the United States. The Mexican republic was falling into disarray, providing little if any governance over conditions in Alta California.

The 1840s saw the beginning of organized immigration westward. The significant work of the overland fur hunters, trappers and traders having come to a close about this same period, many of whom served subsequently as route guides to immigrant parties. Jedediah Smith was the first American "white" person to reach California by overland route in 1826-27. The parties of James Pattie, John Bidwell, George and Jacob Donner, and Joseph Walker were to follow later as overland migrants. Johann Augustus Sutter, who had left Switzerland for America in 1834, arrived in California in 1839, and obtained permission from the Mexican governor to create a colony that he named "New Helvetia" located in the Sacramento Valley near the junction of the Sacramento and American rivers, not far from the site of the future gold discovery. In 1841 ·Sutter purchased the defunct Russian experimental colony named "Fort Ross" located on the bluff overlooking the ocean a few miles north of Bodega Bay. Fort Ross was originally erected by the expeditionary official Kuskof and dedicated on September 10, 1812.

President Monroe, on December 2, 1823, announced what came to be labeled "The Monroe Doctrine," which embodied his Western expansion policy. Among other things, it included American foreign policy sentiments that the continent was no longer to be a convenient subject for colonization by European powers. At the time Russian incursions via Alaska southward to Bodega Bay had already occurred including the colonization and construction of Fort Ross. President Jackson followed with a diplomatic program on the part of the United States to gain possession of the province, as did President Tyler during his administration. Waddy Thompson, United States minister to Mexico under Tyler, summed up the advisability and the need of securing California by speaking of it as the "richest, the most beautiful, and healthiest country in the world." He described the Bay of San Francisco as strategically located and "capacious enough to receive the navies of all the world". Thompson further advised that the control of this bay and that of Monterey and San Diego harbors would give to the United States the needed ports for her merchant and naval vessels and virtual monopoly of the Pacific Ocean. President Polk was elected in 1844 on a platform favoring the annexations of Texas and the settlements of Oregon and Alta California. For the latter purposes Polk created official relations with Thomas Oliver Larkin in Monterey to prepare groundwork for annexation. Thomas O. Larkin, a New England merchant, came to Monterey in 1832, becoming the first American resident rapidly building up a prosperous business. In 1844 he had been appointed United States consul to California by President Polk and served as confidant and publicity agent in connection with American annexation interest.

Along with the foreign policy and diplomatic fronts, the U.S. government sponsored expeditions for exploring routes westward to the Pacific coast and California in support of the cause of annexation and settlement. There had been two major efforts: the first led by Lieutenant Charles Wilkes as a naval exploration expedition from 1838 to 1842 and that of John C. Fremont as an overland surveying exploration expedition to the Rocky Mountains and to Oregon and Northern California from 1842 to 1844. Both of these expeditions were equipped with scientific personnel providing accurate accounts of routes, chartings of bays and other scientific geological and botanical data as well as reporting on population demographics, military impotence and lack of governance.

John Fremont, a naturalist, explorer, scientist and government representative, arrived back in California, with Kit Carson as his guide, on his second expedition in 1844. This time he was to play a major role in negotiating the terms of annexation with Andres Pico creating the "Cahuenga Capitulation" document of January 13, 1847, which effectively ended the Mexican War from California's perspective. This event was antecedent to the Treaty of Guadalupe Hidalgo, signed on February 2, 1848, by which California formally became a part of the United States.

Just a few weeks before this historic treaty event, on January 24, 1848, another occurred. The General Contractor James W. Marshall, along with his construction foreman, Peter Wimmer, chanced upon some glittering particles in the tailrace of a newly constructed sawmill at Coloma, a valley in the foothills of the Sierra Nevada on the South Fork of the American River, belonging to his employer, John A. Sutter. "Gold had been found".[2] Concern over the impact upon his colony Sutter, with the assistance of Marshall, attempted to conceal the find. Rumors and whispers began to be reported in newspapers. Then on May 12, 1848, Sam Brannan, for unclear motives, gathered a crowd while making his way up Montgomery Street in San Francisco in the direction of Portsmouth Square with gold nuggets and dust sack in hand waving and shouting out "Gold! Gold! Gold! from the American River," igniting the "fever." Thus began the "stampede" from the world over and everything changed in California's way of life.

In 1835 Captain W. A. Richardson had laid the foundation for the modern San Francisco by erecting a small crude shelter on the beach known as Yerba Buena. He was followed by,

Jacob P. Lees, who built a substantial wood frame house near the same site. He then added a store and made the place into a trading center for ships putting into port for supplies and repairs. Later, he sold it to the Hudson Bay Company that thereafter this facility became the chief commercial factor in the development of the village. In 1847, the year after Captain Montgomery raised the American flag on July 8, 1846, in the plaza named "Portsmouth Square" in honor of his ship, the name of the area on the western shore of the Bay was formally change from Yerba Buena to San Francisco by the first American mayor (alcalde) Lieutenant Washington A. Bartlett. By 1848 the areas population was approaching nine hundred inhabitants. In December 1846 the first newspaper was printed by its founder and owner Samuel Brannan called the California Star. Brannon's paper rivaled Monterey's The Californian which had begun publication in August of the same year, and owned by Robert Colton and Robert Semple. The first public school was opened and the area increased its commercial activities to also rival that of Monterey.

On February 2, 1848, California passed out of possession of Mexico into the sovereign control of the United States with the formal recognition of the Treaty of Guadalupe Hidalgo. The State Constitutional Convention was held in the newly constructed two-story Colton Hall schoolhouse in Monterey, starting on September 3, 1849, and closing on October 13, 1849. The produced constitutional proposal received ratification by popular unanimous vote on November 13, 1849, leading to California entering the Union, by an act of the United States Congress on September 9, 1850, Admission Day, as the thirty-first state.

The period from 1850 to 1870 saw San Francisco change from "pueblo" and "trading post" into a major metropolis. With the announcement of gold, San Francisco became the most rapidly growing city in the world, enlarging its population from 812 persons in 1847 to twenty-five thousand persons by 1850. From 1850 more than thirty-six thousand immigrants, representing every race, creed and culture, arrived in San Francisco by sea alone. San Francisco, consisting of several settlements, now merged into one. During the Civil War years, the interruption of the flow of goods from the Eastern states drove the development of local industries and converted the harbor of San Francisco into an exporting center. The economy was outgrowing the primitive economy of its frontier days with the investment of Eastern capital into the commercial development of California. The completion of the transcontinental railroad was a major contributing factor to this expansion.

On July 1, 1862, President Lincoln signed a bill authorizing aid in the construction of a railroad and a telegraph line from the Missouri River to the Pacific Ocean, a result of explorations and surveys contained in the Pacific Railroad report submitted in 1855. Congress passed the "Pacific Railroad Bill" providing special government subsidies for private construction ventures in the same year. The Central Pacific Railroad Company founded in June 28, 1861, began work on the California territory portion of the proposed transcontinental railroad line in 1863. Completion of the transcontinental railroad occurred in 1869 with the joining of the Atlantic with the Pacific steel rails and the last spike driven at Promontory Point Utah on May 9th.[3]

The urban growth of California toward the end of the nineteenth century was directly connected with this event. A new flood of population descended upon the state from 1870 to 1890 with more than two hundred thousand persons arriving in California by railroad alone.

Charles Morgan, an engineer by training, had traveled for business purposes to San Francisco via a vessel around

Cape Horn in 1867. Immediately struck by the opportunities for wealth making, particularly in minerals, and the extraordinary beauty of the natural environment of the San Francisco Bay Area, he committed himself to return. He proceeded to do so with his new wife Eliza Parmelee Morgan in 1870 using the newly completed transcontinental railroad as transportation. The birth of their daughter, Julia Morgan, occurred in San Francisco two years later in 1872.

By the 1870s the "pioneer frontier" phase of California history generally was over and broader cultural growth was imminent. The great decline that followed the Gold Rush was to witness resurgence with the discovery, in Nevada, of silver deposits known as the "Comstock Lode" in 1870. California provided the miners, supplies and much of the financing. In 1873 silver production reached its peak and then slumped sharply creating a national financial panic in 1873 with the failure of banks, which in turn set off a flurry of bankruptcies. By 1880 the Comstock rewards were over, although mining activities in California still surpassed those of all Western states. However, by the turn of the century the great wealth accumulated among successful, prominent and powerful persons began to find its way into public projects and support of the growth of the arts and sciences and their institutions. It is also at this time that the newly developing economic middle class of permanent residents in the San Francisco Bay Area began to provide social stability out of which to insist on reform of political governance, elimination of corruption, greater fairness in work practices, and created general pressures for improvement of public moral standards.

At the beginning of the new century, on April 18, 1906, the great earthquake struck the Bay Area necessitating the virtual rebuilding of the city of San Francisco and causing expansion and growth of neighboring communities around the Bay Area and southward to Monterey and Carmel. A new building boom was under way and the decades from 1910 through the 1930s experienced growth and prosperity. Despite the national depression California's commercial activities increased. These were the decades in which Asilomar was founded by the YWCA, in Pacific Grove on Monterey Bay, and its facilities constructed over a period of years, with Julia Morgan as its sole architect.

San Francisco Waterfront Scene in 1849.

The Customs House, Monterey, in 1885

Mission San Carlos Borromeo, Carmel in 1880

Appendix B

The Ecole des Beaux-Arts in Paris: Its History and Design Theory

What became in its final form, the Ecole des Beaux-Arts in 1819 emerged from a long and arduous history of institutional transformations. The inaugurating institutions began with the creation of several academies in 1665 by the powerful French minister of state, Jean-Baptiste Colbert, under the kingship of Louis XIV.[1] One among them emerged as the Academe Royal d'Architecture "officially" established in 1671.[2]

In founding these academies, Colbert sought to realize state interests in several sectors. Among them were increasing financial and military strength, enhancing the status of the royal court, and improving the cultural standing of France. But his overall underlying interest for creating the academies was as a means toward radically reforming all sectors of France's economy through converting the nation's varied processes of production into an industrial mercantilism, which had been successfully developing in other nation-states. The reorganization of the country's entire economy required that the role of the state be central and dominant in order to impose a rigorous and effective control over the effort. The regime sought to lock all private

independent activities into state regulations giving priority
and control to the state enterprise, especially that of
manufacturing, as well as foreign trade. In this overall effort
the production of buildings was seen to be a crucially
significant sector to be reorganized and transformed.

The Royal Academy of Architecture was established on
the basis of a perception that new norms of design and new
construction techniques were needed for the production of
buildings. These distinctively new norms and techniques were
to be sought in and derived from the emerging empirical
techniques of "scientific" observation of nature and not just,
as in the past, accepting and adopting "ancient forms" on the
basis of their "historical authority." As we shall see, these
two approaches would set up a problematic tension to be
played out over the course of the academy's long history under
its various names.

It became the assigned task of the royal architectural
academicians to seek and develop acceptable, coherent and
systematic rules for design, which could be incorporated into
state regulations. The most significant social and institutional
changes involved in this reformation meant converting from
the traditional guild form of organization and development
of labor as a single apprentice task, separating it into two
distinctively training tasks, the role of the designer from that
of the construction laborer. Within the guild system, the
manual and the theoretical aspects of architecture were fused
into a single learning effort. The guildsman acquired both
construction techniques and design principles at the same
time. With the inception of the royal academy, education was
to undergo a radical change. The newly formed academy
offered a form of education that was purely theoretical. No
training in manual construction techniques was included in
the curriculum, thereby separating the realm of design from
that of labor and construction skills. Academic architectural

training was for the first time to be limited to the learning of abstract principles of design.

The Royal Academy of Architecture as a formal institution was actually an outgrowth of a somewhat informal council formed by Colbert in 1665 to furnish building design advice and construction support in service to the royal court's building programs. This goal was to be accomplished by bringing the most eminent architects together in regular meetings to study and exchange ideas, collect, improve and record existing knowledge and to solve pressing architectural problems. An added element to this goal was that members of the council were charged with giving informal public lectures on the theory of architecture with the aim of cultivating public interest. It was in connection with these lectures, almost as an accidental byproduct, that the first school solely devoted to training architects evolved and eventually achieved worldwide fame and influence. The informal open public lectures soon became regularized into formal "courses" having a cycle lasting two or more years and attended by audiences who mostly consisted of persons aspiring to become architectural practitioners. The new school received the state's official recognition, under various names, and support continuously from 1671 to its closure in 1968, with the exception of a period of "repression" during the French revolutionary period.

The import of including the term "academy" in the overall title of the school was intended at the time to convey two ideas: First, to establish the sense of being a prestigious "society of distinguished rank" and second, to indicate an organized institute as a "place of study and learning" (for this latter sense, see Chapter 2). The term "academy," in its "social rank" sense, had the effect of raising the architect to the status of being a kind of philosopher-teacher of architectural theory, and, as well, indicating a distinguished elite class associated with the royal court.

As we shall see, throughout the existence of the French academic architectural tradition the continuously dominant theory of design, despite the presence of other approaches, derived primarily from classical ideals. Architecture from this perspective was considered for the most part as a "fine" art. Academic training emphasized formal design interests featuring the study of composition and principles of proportion aimed at evolving universal rules for the realization of beauty of form. It was thought that fixed universal rules were discoverable through devoted systematic measurement of the great masterpieces to be found primarily in the Italian Renaissance and the antecedent period of classical Roman antiquity.

The ordering principles of design to be found in the canonical works of these periods were those identified as being generally accepted by the foremost among those personages "best qualified" to judge their merit. Those best qualified to judge merit were intelligent, learned, persons who had already demonstrated their abilities by their own works and writings. Thus "universal consent" by authority of a certain recognized elite was deemed the test of quality and thereby excellence. Within the institution of the academy, this authority fell to the faculty of appointed professors who managed to sustain their collective view through control of student competitions and the related jury system for which they wrote the programs and awarded prizes.

Most of these views were manifested at the outset in the first formal meeting and the subsequent series of meetings dealing with the formation of the academy held in December 1671. In the first meeting Nicholas Francois-Blondel, its first appointed director, announced that the mission of the academy would be to formulate principles of architecture and, secondly, to teach doctrine based on them. The follow up meetings were devoted to the problem of good taste, the outcome of which was the collective statement that "the veritable rule for recognizing things of good taste among those that are pleasing is to consider what has always been more pleasing to intelligent persons, whose merit has been demonstrated by their work or by their writings."[3] The rules of architectural design were de facto assumed to be discoverable, confirmable and teachable.

However, at the early stage of the establishment of the Royal Academy of Architecture there emerged contending views reflecting different approaches to architecture. A permanent tension arose between the views held by two basic groups, each with their own internal divergences. These two groups of allegiances became habitually known as the "ancients," who were the conservatives, and the "moderns," who were the progressivists.

The "modern" oriented theoreticians generally held that good architecture is in direct accord with the nature of materials, structural techniques, suitability to purpose and relative to the time and place of its construction. They advocated direct expression of these factors in the building's character. Historical reference, elaborate ornamentation and the ideal of beauty as the ultimate aim, tended to be downplayed but not entirely dismissed. Building conceptions were to be based on the need to maximize utility and minimize cost. Laws of design were to be legitimized by rationally inferred causal factors backed by empirical tests. The aim was to bring a certain mathematical rigor of method to building design outcomes, much on the model, for example, of that required for designing bridge structures. However, the attempt to empirically establish formal and symbolic aesthetic effects of buildings through the mathematical method in the same manner as an engineer, which is as a form of "mechanics," was to be crucially problematic for this orientation.

The "ancients" theoreticians generally held to the view that good architecture is one that is ordered by a criteria of ideal proportions latent in and warranted by the authority of the great masterworks of the Renaissance and antiquity. The method of gaining insight in these was to be found by searching historical records and by conducting archeological field measurements. The "ancients" thought in absolutist and idealist conceptual terms of beauty, composition, proportion, axial symmetry, contrast, repetition, scale and variety. They advocated the primacy of aesthetic criteria of design over the practical. The plastic formal and decorative features of buildings were to be conditioned by these criteria. Purposefulness, efficiency, adaptability, the role of materials and climates, cultural and physical contexts were downplayed, if not ignored. The absence of intuitive agreement on the rules of design or of "correct taste" was to be crucially problematic, as well, for this orientation.

The tensions and conflicts of these two major trends, which also involved the two other conflicting positions of academies versus guilds and technology versus classicism, resulted not only in a divergence in concepts of architectural education, but curiously resulted in an eclectic approach in architecture. This kind of eclecticism was marked, by generating an almost infinite number of styles, where any individual building may follow a single style or combinations of styles. Eclecticism tended to waver between either imitating single examples from the past or studying many classical examples in order to compositionally combine the best features of those selected that would result in meeting "correct" taste.

Consequently, the tensions set up between history and nature as authorities, economics and beauty as ideals, and intuition and rational inference as forms of knowledge became the foremost issues influencing not only academic thought but also its institutions. What evolved through the course of transformations was a split: on the one hand there is the designer-engineer orientation and on the other there is the artist-architect. By the beginning of the eighteenth century the approach to design was already bifurcating into two seemingly irreconcilable directions: design developed as a science and design developed as an art. This split carried over from its theoretical form to the very institutions themselves. Out of the "progessivist" orientation, special schools of engineering emerged as independent institutions around 1740. The founding of the Ecole de Polytechnic is the most significant, where building design is represented basically as a technical science. The approach to architecture maintained by the "ancients" who viewed it as a "fine art" eventually would be served by the newly named Ecole des Beaux-Arts arising out of the hiatus during the French Revolution. Within the academies, the overall organization of all the differing art forms inevitably became a subject of much discussion. The claims for prestige among the individual arts were a major motivating factor. In 1746, Abbe Batteux formulated a systematic categorization of the arts, based on a separation of the "Fine Arts" (pleasurable arts) from the "Mechanical Arts" (useful Arts), which became very influential. He had ambivalent feelings about where to locate architecture, it being a 'mixed art' in his scheme.[4] This was one dilemma that would lead to further efforts to recast his proffered system.

The eighteenth century saw a major shift in the attitudes about architecture. France had taken up the mood for science stemming from the ideas of Francis Bacon followed by Rene Descartes and others. The new ideas and tendencies generated by the Romantic movement and the emerging effects of the Industrial Revolution both complicated and coerced modifications of the traditionally "strict classicism" approach and its connection with "correct taste." These new influences led to "free style eclecticism" and its connection

with "appropriate taste," at its most flexible stage by the end
of the nineteenth century.

The principal concerns of architecture until this time had
been with the formation of symbolic and formal aesthetic
criteria, tied mainly to religious and monumental civic building
interests. With the shift in cultural climate and the emergence
of new building types, architects were now drawn to respect
functional needs, construction and the role of materials. They
came to place greater stress upon the need for a "rational"
approach to buildings that included these practical interests,
along with traditional formalist attitudes and its interest in
purely plastic affects. Architectural theory shifted from being
solely a theoretical formalism to include theoretical
pragmatism, seeking a comfortable compromise between the
demands of form and the dictates of useful efficiency. Thus,
beginning with the founding of the royal academy to its
reinstitution under the name of L' Ecole des Beaux-Arts the
key legitimizing term "rational" does not remain a monolithic
univocal theory pure and simple, but undergoes a contentious
struggle of shifting content of considerable complexity over
two and a half centuries.

The first director of the Royal Academy of Architecture,
appointed in 1671 by Colbert under the King's auspices, was
Nicholas Francois-Blondel, an architect, engineer and
mathematician. Francois-Blondel, characterized as having a
Platonist temperament, pressed his own doctrinal imprint on
the new academy at the outset of its formation. That doctrine
was the "strict classicism" ideal harbored by the "ancients."
A contemporary of Francois-Blondel's was Claude Perault, a
practitioner of architecture who designed the East facade of
the Louvre in 1667. Perault was an outspoken influential
theoretician. He had translated with commentary the writings
of Vitruvius, and became known as a "progressivist" opponent
to Francois-Blondel's views.

It was not until Jacques Francois-Blondel, a distant cousin of the first director, was appointed director of the academy in 1762 that "strict classicism" began to be significantly challenged. He was familiar with the views of Perault and introduced a somewhat less absolutist view into the doctrinal status quo of the academy. While holding to a respect for "tradition," he urged that historical masterpieces should not be simply copied, but needed to be understood as "circumstantially conditioned" and "eclectically adapted" to new situations. He held that human needs, customs and politics change, that lands and climates differ, and consequently architects needed to create different types of architecture using different materials and methods. Jacques Francois-Blondel, nevertheless, advocated the traditional requirements of attending to composition, proportion and symmetry. But at the same time he directed attention to practicality, believing that architecture is much more than just a matter of beauty and proportion based on an academic notion of abstract principle. He thought architecture to be a combination of practicality and character requiring a great flexibility in approach. Despite the academic debate as to whether beauty was an absolute constant or subject to change conditioned by circumstance, the overriding approach remained fundamentally that of eclecticism. This was mainly and famously sought through the rigorous study of the proportions of the Classical "Five Orders."[5]

The "building arts" underwent a radical technological reorientation in the late eighteenth century coinciding with the Industrial Revolution. The curriculum shifted to include not only theoretical issues but also increased an emphasis on construction interests. Technical aspects of buildings, such as the behavior of materials, began to gain greater emphasis. The introduction and availability of a new material called iron, with its unique physical properties, together with the developments in mathematical science of materials and

structures, eventually induced new views toward architectural
form.[6] In this respect "building could no longer be treated as
an art or a craft; it had to become a branch of theoretical and
applied science."[7] The new "mechanics" of building materials
placed "The behavior of loaded structural members on a
systematic and theoretical basis."[8]

At the time of the French Revolution the royal academy
waned. Napoleon Bonaparte's reforms involved the need
for many new building types to accommodate new civic and
military programs. Napoleon supported the founding of the
Ecole des Polytechnic. The creation of this school at once
institutionalized technology and science and dethroned the
royal academy as a bastion of conservatism, formalism,
historicism, and academics. Its staff was made up primarily
of civil engineers along with some architects, one of whom
was N. Durand. In 1795 Durand was appointed professor at
the Ecole de Polytechnic, which was to "replace" the old
Royal Academy of Architecture.[9] Durand's theories and
teachings acquired great significance. He advocated that
architecture should concern itself exclusively with utilitarian
aspect of buildings. For him construction was the only
important concept, thus, unseating the traditional primacy
of aesthetic criteria of design. For Durand the workings of
structural principles in respect of achieving an organization
of space leads logically and automatically to establishing a
compositional system and an aesthetic outcome. Form is
therefore derived mainly from structural interests. Durand's
'rationalism' nevertheless remains compatible and supportive
of historical classicism. The distinctive feature is with the
flexibility of "style adaptation" within his eclecticism. He
allows stylistic features the role of being the dynamic and
interchangeable aspects of design. Despite Durand's
rationalist modifications, "eclecticism" remains the
paramount notion conditioning the conceptions of
architecture.

With these events the royal academy symbolized the bastion of conservatism where methods and subjects of teaching reflected "elitist neglect," harboring a disregard of events and problems of present reality and future anticipation. It showed a virtual lack of interest in or knowledge of modern developments in materials and structural design techniques, and of the emergence of many new building types. Nor did it recognize the outmoding of the use of ornamental details. But with Napoleon Bonaparte's abdication in 1814 the royalist element of the academy sought a reversion to the pre-revolutionary way of life and culture. Louis XVIII revived the old Royal Academy of Architecture, but reorganized and reinstated it under the now famous name of L' Ecole des Beaux-Arts. Quatremere De Quincy was appointed to oversee the school and proceeded to impose upon its curriculum and practice a program of narrow and doctrinaire formalist ideals based strictly on Roman antiquity.

The period of the Roman monumental style prevailed through the 1850s, until Henry Labrouste was appointed to the Ecole in 1867. He became a key figure in a revolt against a narrow "classical rationalism" advocating instead a "free classicism." Labrouste argued that architecture must be connected with social usefulness and incorporate technological advances and new materials. He established his own independent atelier, which was active from 1830 to 1846. Despite the innovations he espoused and practiced, he remained very much a Beaux-Arts architect, utilizing most of the compositional techniques of academic classicism.

Louis Jules André took over Labrouste's independent atelier in one of the most confused and turbulent times at the Ecole. He continued during his appointment, as a "progressivist," to support and teach the "free classicism" advocated by Labrouste. The American architect Henry H. Richardson arrived in Paris and studied at Andre's atelier from

1859 to 1862. Richardson was also greatly influenced by August Vaudremer who, significantly, had inspired inclusion of the Romanesque style into the Ecole's curriculum. Another American architect, Louis Sullivan, arrived in Paris in 1874 to attend the Ecole, but totally disappointed and recoiling from its views, he stayed only for a short while to work for Vaudremer, returning to the United States in the same year.[10]

The Romantic medievalist, Viollet Le Duc, though he did not train at the Ecole, was appointed professor in 1867. In that year he gave a lecture in which students, by apparent prearrangement, and supported by a faction of the faculty, protested the views he was advocating by marching one by one out of the hall while clapping. Le Duc was immediately dismissed on the basis of this event. Nevertheless, during his stay, he had introduced Gothic revivalism and structural determinism that forced the conservative "ancients" to compromise the traditional training in "classical orders" by incorporating the study of gothic structure into the curriculum. This event led eventually to the introduction of the first formal course in medieval architecture taught by Henry Lemmonier in 1891.

Bernard Maybeck arrived in Paris in 1881. He entered Louis Jules Andres' atelier toward preparing for entering the Ecole. He was accepted in 1882, ranking twenty-second among the 250 applicants that year, of which only forty were taken. Maybeck was greatly influenced by Lemmonier and Brune as well as Jules André. At the time Emmanuel Brune began teaching a course that presented the emerging mathematical theory of modern structural engineering design.

Julian Gaudet, a pupil of Louis Jules André, was appointed professor at the Ecole in 1894. He became the leading architectural theorist at the Ecole, teaching until 1907. In his lectures on architectural theory, Julian Gaudet advocated: "the axis is the key of a design and will be the key of the composition. In an architectural design it is necessary to proceed before all by means of axes."[11] Gaudet went on to state "in architecture the first studies ought to be essentially classic" and that "symmetry with, however, variety ought generally be sought."[12]

The master-patron architects in charge of the ateliers, which supported the Ecole, truly were the teaching professors of the school, effectively transmitting their sensibilities about architecture directly to students (for this topic, see chapter 2). Master-patrons differed greatly in their teaching methods and their theories were not uniform. Their artistic personalities and interests varied greatly. Consequently, an aspirant had to chose carefully. Nevertheless, the most common element to be found in the approach to building design, namely eclecticism, was sustained by the Ecole itself, through its competition jury system.

When Julia Morgan received her diploma in 1901 and returned to the United States, a fellow student, Tony Garnier, the Grand Prix de Rome winner of 1899, submitted his Rome studies project known as "The Industrial City," which caused great controversy and stress within the institution, engendering unrest that festered on for many years until student riots broke out, causing government closure of the school in 1968. Thus came to an end the singular most influential and longest enduring educational institution in the history of architecture.

APPENDIX C

ASILOMAR'S BUILDINGS AND IMPROVEMENTS DESIGNED BY JULIA MORGAN

Julia Morgan developed an overall site plan for the center in 1912. The designs for the stone pillars or gate posts, serving as entry markers, and the Phoebe Apperson Hearst Multipurpose Social Hall Building were the first two developments, both completed in 1913. These were followed by a support building then known as the Engineer's Cottage, and by sleeping accommodations (later known as "long houses") for 350 persons consisting of wood platforms with canvas tent coverings. Over the next fifteen years buildings, and other improvements were added, all with Julia Morgan as the architect. Modifications have been made to some of Ms. Morgan's buildings, which significantly alter the originally intended practical and aesthetic values from those sought at the time of their design.

1913—Stone Entry Pillars (entry gate marker posts)
1913—Phoebe Apperson Hearst Social Hall (Administration Building)
1913—Ten Canvas Tented Sleeping Platforms (torn down over time, the last in 1971)

1913—Engineer's Cottage

1915—Grace H. Dodge Chapel (also multi-purpose in design)

1915—Guest Inn (torn down in the 1960s)

1916—Martha and Mary Lodge (demolished)

1916—Visitors Lodge (known as the Lodge)

1917—Forty-car-capacity Garage (demolished)

1918—Stuck-up Inn: originally for housing women employees.

1918—Viewpoint Cottage (Health Cottage)

1918—Crocker Dining Hall (remodeled and annex added in 1961)

1919—Scripps Class Hall (burned 1951)

1923—Pirates' Den: originally for housing men employees.

1927—Director's Cottage (demolished 1959)

1927—Pincers (Currently the Director's Cottage)

1927—Scripps Lodge Annex

1928—Merrill Hall (Auditorium)

Note: Some dates are approximate.

Appendix D

Julia Morgan: Chronology

1872—(January 20) Julia Morgan born in San Francisco to Charles and Eliza Morgan.

1873—Family moves permanently to Oakland, California.

1890—Morgan graduates from Oakland High School and enters the University of California, Berkeley.

1894—Graduates from University of California, Berkeley, with Bachelor of Science in civil engineering.

1895—Works and studies with Bernard Maybeck.

1896—Departs for Paris to study architecture; Joins the atelier of Marcel de Monclos.

1898—Becomes first woman accepted to architecture program at Ecole des Beaux-Arts.

1902—Becomes first woman to gain a diploma from the Ecole des Beaux-Arts.

1902—Returns home; works for John Galen Howard as chief designer for the Hearst Mining Building and Greek Theater projects for the University of California at Berkeley.

1903—Designs Campanile and Margaret Carnegie Library for Mills College, Oakland.

1904—Becomes first woman to earn architect's license from state of California. Opens architectural office in the Merchant Exchange Building, San Francisco.

1906—Great San Francisco earthquake; Morgan's office

destroyed. Appointed as architect for the reconstruction of the Fairmont Hotel, San Francisco.

1912—Appointed architect for the YWCA Asilomar Summer Camp facilities, Pacific Grove, California.

1919—Begins work on San Simeon for William Randolph Hearst.

1924—Morgan's father dies.

1929—Julia Morgan's mother dies;receives her honorary doctor of laws degree from the University of California at Berkeley.

1950—Closes architectural office.

1957—(February 2) Dies at the age of eighty-five.

CHAPTER NOTES

Preface:

1. The third largest project in relationship to these two was the development of Phoebe Apperson Hearst's vacation residence "Wyntoon", located on 'The Bend' of the Mcloud River, near Mt. Shasta, California. Originally begun in 1902 it passed into the hands of William Randolph Hearst and suffered a devastating fire in 1929. In the aftermath, he considerably enlarged the number of buildings in the complex retaining Bernard Maybeck and Julia Morgan as architects. Work ceased at the site in 1943.

Introduction:

1. Julia Morgan's secretary, Mrs. Lillian Forney, retained many of her papers and the drawings that were not picked up by clients, or the then building owners, contacted at the closing of the office. Many of these have been retained by or given in turn by Mrs. Forney's daughter, Lynn Forney McMurray, who is one of Julia Morgan's two godchildren, to the Bancroft Special Collections Library and to the College of Environmental Design Archives and Bancroft Libraries at the University of California, Berkeley. Many drawings and personal academic and profession-related effects passed to her nephew, Morgan North, and his wife Flora, and these were subsequently given to the Special Collections Department of the Robert F. Kennedy Library at California Polytechnic State University in San Luis Obispo. Julia Morgan's architectural library was disbursed to un-known parties.

2.   It is the authors understanding that the New York office of the YWCA, the known repository of the records dealing with the purchase and development of Asilomar discarded many of its older files some years ago, the Asilomar files apparently being among them.

3.   The architectural critic for the San Francisco Chronicle, Allan Temko, in his review of Sara Holmes Boutelle's book "Julia Morgan, Architect", opens his review as follows: "The most extraordinary woman in the history of architecture, Julia Morgan, hated being known as a "woman architect". The tiny California spinster considered her personal life and her sex irrelevant to a career that was almost as prolific as that of contemporary, Frank Lloyd Wright".

Julia Morgan: A Biographical Sketch

1.   Another significant figure that developed a considerable reputation in both the design and architectural fields is Mary Colter. A contemporary of Julia Morgan, Mary Colter was born in St. Paul Minnesota in 1869 and died in 1958. She spent her career in architecture practicing in the Southwest as an employee of the Fred Harvey Company whose client was the Santa Fe Railroad Company. She attended the California School of Design in San Francisco from 1887 to 1890 where she trained in the arts program. Having no formal academic training in architecture, she worked as an apprentice for a San Francisco architect while attending the school of design up until her graduation. During this time she lived in Oakland at 1066 10th Street and commuted to San Francisco. After graduation she returned to St Paul and for a while was employed teaching the "Mechanical Arts" until beginning her own independent practice in architecture. Mary Colter practiced in a very different milieu and produced buildings of a very different character than those of Julia Morgan. For Mary Colter's career, see Berke, "Mary Colter: Architect of the Southwest" in the Bibliography.

2.   Oakland was founded in 1850. It began at the edge of Lake Merritt as a hamlet called "Clinton" on land purchased by Patton brothers from Don Luis Peralta, who had held the Spanish grant for the Rancho San Antonio since 1820.

3.   The Women's Athletic Club of San Francisco was organized in 1915. Many of San Francisco's most prominent families were enrolled on the membership list. It functioned, for the most part, as a social club for cultural activities, including sports. The Century Club of California was one of the most exclusive women's clubs of the state. It was founded by Mrs. Phoebe Apperson Hearst in 1888 and formally incorporated in 1904. It was a women's organization devoted to advancing cultural purposes. The membership was limited stipulatively by charter to four thousand persons, these drawn from the state's most prominent citizens. Julia Morgan was a lifetime member. She was commissioned in 1914 to remodel the club's building at 1355 Franklin Street in San Francisco.

4.   Further to this point, see the Author's "Julia Morgan's Architectural Presence on the Monterey Peninsula" listed in the Bibliography.

5.   Personal correspondence from J. Morgan to LeBruns, dated July 19, 1897, Special Collections, Kennedy Library, California Polytechnic State University.

6.   Personal correspondence from J. Morgan to LeBruns, dated Dec. 12, 1897, Special Collections, Kennedy Library, California Polytechnic State University.

7.   Quoted variously. See, for example, Julia Morgan by Ginger Wadsworth, 43.

8.   For substantiation of this view, see Taylor Coffman's wonderful and informative book "Building for Hearst and Morgan: Voices from the George Loorz Papers".

The Ecole des Beaux-Arts: Architectural Training in Paris

1.   Personal correspondence, J. Morgan to the LeBruns, July 19, 1897, Special Collections, Kennedy Library, California Polytechnic State University.

2.   Ibid.

3.   Ibid.

4.   Ibid.

5.   Personal correspondence, J. Morgan to the LeBruns, May 30, 1898, Special Collections, Kennedy Library, California Polytechnic State University.

6.   Ibid.

7.   Personal correspondence, J. Morgan to the LeBruns, December 12, 1897, Special Collections, Kennedy Library, California Polytechnic State University.

The Arts and Crafts Movement: English Origins and the San Francisco Bay Region's Unique Version

1.   Ernest A. Batchelder, "The Arts and Crafts Movement in America," The Craftsman, vol. 16 (August 1909), 544.

2.   Charles Keeler, The Simple Home. See bibliography.

The San Francisco Bay Region: Emerging Technologies and Institutions in the Formative Years

1.   John F. Morse, quoted in Great Citizen (A Biography of William H. Crocker) by David W. Rider, Historical Publications (San Francisco: 1962), 14.

2. The name "Hayward Lumber Co." is still in use at the lumberyard adjacent to Asilomar Conference Center at Sunset and Crocker streets. Dolbeer's invention took on different forms in its application, but its thrust was to replace the use of oxen teams to drag rough cut logs from timber sites to train sites or local saw mill sites.

3. Susanna Riess, "The Work of Walter Steilberg and Julia Morgan," The Julia Morgan Architectural Project, vol. 1, Bancroft Library, University of California Regional Oral History Office (1976), 131.

4. Francois Hennebique and Henry Labrouste were early experimental architects in France with architectural concrete, along with August Perret. See Kenneth Frampton Tectonic Culture, Peter Collins's Concrete: the Vision of a New Architecture.

Julia Morgan's Two Largest Projects: The Hearst Castle and Asilomar Compared

1. Susanna Riess, "The Work of Walter Steilberg and Julia Morgan," The Julia Morgan Architectural Project, vol. 1, Bancroft Library, University of California Regional Oral History Office (1976), 56

2. James Cary, Julia Morgan, 77.

3. William Randolph Hearst Jr., The Hearsts: Father & Son, 69.

4. Ibid., 70.

5. Susanna Riess, "The Work of Walter Steilberg and Julia Morgan," The Julia Morgan Architectural Project, vol. 1, Bancroft Library, University of California Regional Oral History Office (1976), 23.

6. William Randolph Hearst Jr., The Hearsts: Father & Son, 72.

7.   Susanna Riess, "The Work of Walter Steilberg and Julia Morgan,"
     The Julia Morgan Architectural Project, vol. 1, Bancroft Library,
     University of California Regional Oral History Office (1976), 61.

8.   For full insight on this point, see Taylor Coffman's, "Building for
     Hearst and Morgan: Voices from the George Loorz Papers'.

9.   Susanna Riess, "The Work of Walter Steilberg and Julia Morgan,"
     The Julia Morgan Architectural Project, vol. 1, Bancroft Library,
     University of California Regional Oral History Office (1976), 90.

The Site of Asilomar, Pacific Grove:
The Origins of a Monterey Bay Township

1.   After it opened in June 1880, the majestic setting and elaborate
     facilities of the Hotel Del Monte soon became known worldwide.
     People of wealth from all over the world traveled to stay at the
     resort. Two train trips were made daily to and from San Francisco, a
     three-and-one-half-hour run. There were also special track sidings
     to accommodate those who chose to come with their own private
     railroad cars. Located within a mile of the old capital of Monterey,
     it was built at the cost of $1 million dollars and in a time span of one
     hundred days. The buildings were classically elaborate Victorian
     architecture covering 126 acres of cultivated park like grounds
     accommodating four hundred guests. The guest constituency, were
     mostly the wealthy, prominent and famous.

The Asilomar Conference Grounds:
The Manner and Course of Its Founding

1.   At the time of its dissolution, Samuel F. B. Morse, namesake great
     grandson of the inventor of the Morse Code, was a manager with
     the Pacific Improvement Co. Upon Charles Crocker's death, Morse
     was appointed to oversee the liquidation of the company's assets
     that were distributed between the surviving Crocker family, the
     University of California and Stanford University. Morse joined with

Mortimer Fleishhacker, the president of the Great Western Paper Co., located in Woodside, California, to purchase out of the company the remaining undeveloped land in the area including Del Monte Forest lands. From this purchase they created the Del Monte Properties Company, which remains in operational existence to this day.

2. The offer for free land in Carmel was likely made by the real estate developer James F. Devendorf. Devendorf and his partner, Frank Powers, had purchased the land to be known as Carmel-by-the-Sea, from Santiago Duckworth who, in 1888, had acquired the acreage out of the existing Las Manzantias Ranch. At the time, Duckworth had already gained county-approval for a plan to develop a community, likely inspired by the growing success of the Methodist community of Pacific Grove. Mrs. Abbie J. Hunter, a real estate investment professional from San Francisco later joined Duckworth's venture. It was she who apparently gave the name "Carmel-by-the Sea" to the village area. Devendorf and Powers formed the Carmel Development Company in 1902 and began promoting sales. In 1905 Stanford University President, David Starr Jordan purchased property and built a house, to be followed by other faculty, including many from the University of California at Berkeley. The 1906 earthquake sent a stream of "refugees" from the Bay Area, some of whom remained permanently. Beginning about 1910 Devendorf undertook a major campaign to attract a population to Carmel which may have been the context in which his offer was made.

3. Quoted from "The Story of Asilomar," undated pamphlet, Pat Hathaway Collection, California Views, Monterey. No. 436-PH074

Asilomar's Julia Morgan Buildings: Artistically Considered

1. Sally Woodbridge, "Introduction" to Susanna Reiss, Julia Morgan Architectural History Project, vol. 1, vi.

2. Quoted in Susanna Riess, Julia Morgan Architectural History Project, vol. 1, 88.

3. Julia Morgan utilized the "circular" or "oval" scheme at San Simeon, Mills College in Oakland, Wyntoon in Lake Tahoe, and at Asilomar.

Julia Morgan's Buildings: Experientially Considered

1. The "basilica" form, having clerestory windows as a major feature, has a long architectural tradition as a building type going back to ancient Greek times when wood structures were built as public assembly halls.

2. Quoted in Susanna Riess, Julia Morgan Architectural History Project, vol. 1, 85.

2. Ibid., 86.

Concluding Remarks

1. Reflective of the importance and sensitivity Julia Morgan possessed concerning 'composition', she is known to have remarked on occasions about her concern over the "asymmetry" of her own facial appearance which had come to manifest some disfiguration attributable to the mastoid infection that she suffered from.

2. Allan Temko, "The Mystery of Julia Morgan", See Bibliography.

Appendix A

1. The Spanish explorations of the times were part of the worldwide quest for "gold and El Dorados" by nations that were pressed to sustain or enhance their treasuries and power, driven by the attractions of "myth and avarice" to en-join "dreams with

conquests." See, for example, Rush for Riches by J. Holliday, especially pages 3-5.

2. The original gold nugget piece found in the tailrace of Sutter's mill, is known as the "Wimmer Nugget" apparently due to Elizabeth Wimmer having performed the initial chemical tests on the nugget in her kitchen to confirm that it was in fact gold and also having retained it in her possession. This nugget is housed in the Bancroft Library at the University of California, Berkeley.

3. The historic ceremonial "Golden Spike", the last spike to be driven at Promontory Point, in the Territory of Utah, at the completion of the meeting of the track between the Union Pacific and the Central Pacific portions on May 10, 1869, is housed in the Cantor Art Center, formally the Leland Stanford Junior Museum, Stanford, California.

Appendix B

1. The earliest forerunner and the first academy in France prior to those founded by Colbert was the Literary Academe Francaise, established by Richelieu, minister to Louis XIII in 1635. The purpose of this academy was to bring order to and regulate the French language and develop standard dictionary and grammar reference texts.

2. The founding of the Academe Royal D'Architecture represented historical ties that had genesis reaching back to the academies of philosophy, literature art and science of the Italian Renaissance and in turn to those of antiquity. The term "academy" was adopted from the philosophy school that Plato conducted in a garden near Athens known by that name. One of the earliest important schools in Italy was the Academy Platonica founded in Florence around 1470 devoted to philosophy and literature. While the writings of Leonardo da Vinci already suggested that art should be separated from handcrafts, the first school actually setup in opposition to the apprentorship system of the Middle ages appears to have been that

established by Bertoldo di Giovanni for painters and sculptors in Florence in 1490. The Roman architect and author, Vitruvius, had earlier recommended that an architect's training should include a broad liberal education as well as a technical specialization, thereby also indicating a separation between artist and craftsman. The historian, Giorgio Vasari, played a major role in shifting the nature of academies from informal and private meeting groups to definite, formal institutions under the aegis of government, giving them official backing. The Accademia di San Luca was founded under the Medici in Rome in 1593. The purpose of this academy was the education of painters, sculptures and architects. It instituted the giving of prizes to the best students under competitive conditions in 1708. This academy appears to serve in its aim, subjects and structure as the precursor model to those evolved in France.

3. Recorded in "Proceedings of the Royal Academy of Architecture," 1671-1793, ten volumes, cited in Egbert, The Beaux-Arts Tradition in French Architecture.

4. For further details about the historical development of the system of the arts, see Oskar Kristeller's essay "The Modern system of the Arts", Journal of the History of Ideas, vol. 12 (1951), 465-527, vol. 12 (1952),17-46.

5. By the time of Jacque Blondel's appointment to the academy, the increased ability to travel generated archeological and antiquarian interests. History began to be seen as a catalogue of changing styles from which to eclectically develop building designs. This, together with the extraordinary expansion in the publication of printed materials, led to the formation of an architectural literature disseminating a large quantity of knowledge and images that become the resource tool for students of the past to learn "correct" taste and later "appropriate" taste. Library collections became very important to the learning and practice of architecture. Julian D. LeRoy, appointed as adjunct professor to Blonde, was an antiquarian and a major cultivator and caretaker of the academy's library

resources. LeRoy also pursued archeological field measurement work and was the first to introduce Greek architecture to the academy, which in his time was largely unknown.

6. In 1792, the Royal Academy of Science completed the creation of the metric system that was adopted by the state as the standard measurement tool. This system, some 105 years later, was to cause Julia Morgan considerable frustration as an "aspirant" taking the examinations to qualify for entering the Ecole.

7. Carl Condit, American Building (Chicago University Press, 1968), 77.

8. Ibid., 78.

9. The Ecole des Polytechnic actually coexisted parallel with the then "suppressed" royal academy. The royal academy would be reorganized, combining sculpture, painting and architecture, and given a new name: L' Ecole des Beaux-Arts.

10. Some other American architects of note who attended L' Ecole des Beaux-Arts beyond those mentioned in this Appendix, were Richard Morris Hunt (the first to attend in 1846), Addison Mizner, John Stewardson, John Mervin Carrere and Thomas Hastings.

11. Julian Gaudet, Element et Theorie de L'Architecture, vol. 1 (1901- 1904), 40-41.

12. Ibid., vol. 1, 28.

BIBLIOGRAPHY

Aidala, Thomas. *Hearst Castle, San Simeon.* New York: Hudson Hill Press, 1981.

___. *"Asilomar."* Architectural Review 157 (February 1975): 123.

Armstrong, Jane. *"Woman Architect Who Helped Build the Fairmont Hotel."* The Architect and Engineer of California (October 1907): 69-71.

Ashbee, Charles. *Should We Stop Teaching Art.* London: Batsford Press, 1911.

Baker, Paul R. Stanny: *The Guilded Life of Stanford White.* New York: Free Press, 1989.

Benton, Tim, and Charlotte Benton. *Form and Function: A Source Book for the History of Architecture and Design 1890-1939.* London: Crosby Lockwood Staples, 1975.

Berke, Arnold. *Mary Colter: Architect of the Southwest.* New York: Princeton Architectural Press, 2002.

Boutelle, Sara Holmes. *Julia Morgan, Architect.* New York: Abbeville Press, 1988.

___. *"Julia Morgan." Master Builders.* Maddex, ed. Washington, DC: Preservation Press, 1985.

Browning, P. *To the Golden Shore: America Goes to California—1849*. Lafayette, CA: Great West Books, 1995.

Cardwell, Kenneth. *Bernard Maybeck: Artisan, Artist, Architect*. Santa Barbara, CA: Peregrine Smith, 1977.

Case, Victoria, and Robert Case. *We Called it Culture (History of Chautauquas)*. New York: Doubleday, 1948.

Caughey, John W. *California*. 2nd ed. Englewood Cliffs, NJ: Prentice Hall, 1953.

Caughey, J., and Laree Caughey, Eds. *California Heritage: An Anthology of History Literature*. Los Angeles, CA: Ward Ritchie Press, 1962.

Cleland, Robert G. *A History of California*. New York: Macmillan Company, 1939.

Cobden-Sanderson, T. J. *The Arts and Crafts Movement*. Hammersmith Publication Society, 1805.

Coffman, Taylor. *Hearst Castle: The Story of William Randolph Hearst and San Simeon*. Santa Barbara: Sequoia Communications, 1985.

Coffman, Taylor. *Building for Hearst and Morgan: Voices from the George Loorz Papers*. Berkeley, CA: Berkeley Hills Books, 2003.

Collins, Peter. *Concrete: The Vision of a New Architecture*. New York: Horizon Press, 1959.

Cumming, E., and W. Kaplan. *The Arts and Crafts Movement*. New York: Thames & Hudson, 1991.

Condit, Carl W. *American Building Art*. 2 vols. London: Oxford University Press, 1960.

____. *American Building*. Chicago: University of Chicago Press, 1968.

Cram, Ralph. *"The influence of the French School on American Architecture."* Journal of the Proceedings of the AIA, 1899.

____. *"The Case against the Ecole des Beaux-Arts."* American Architect & Building News. Vol. 14, no. 1096 (December 1896): 107-9.

Davey, Peter. *Architecture of the Arts and Crafts Movement*. New York: Rizzoli, 1980.

Drexeler, Arthure. *The Architecture of the Ecole Des Beaux-Arts*. Museum of Modern Art, 1975.

Dunning, Glenna. *"Julia Morgan." Architectural Series: Bibliography (A1880)*, August 1987.

Egbert, Donald. *The Beaux-Arts Tradition in French Architecture*. Princeton, NJ: Princeton University Press, 1980.

Eldrege, Zoeth S. *The Beginnings of San Francisco*. San Francisco Press, 1912.

Elliot, Cecil D. *Technics and Architecture*. Massachusetts Institute of Technology Press, 1992.

Failing, Patricia. *"She Was America's Most Successful Woman-Architect and Hardly Anybody Knows Her Name."* Art News. Vol. 80 (January 1981): 66-71.

Field, Walker. *"A Re-examination into the Invention of the Balloon Frame."* Journal of the Society of Architectural Historians. Vol. 2 (October 1942): 3-29.

Flagg, Ernest. *"The Ecole Des Beaux-Arts"* (Parts I to III). Architectural Record (January to March, 1894).

Frampton, Kenneth. *Tectonic Culture: The Poetics of Construction in Nineteenth and Twentieth-Century Architecture.* Massachusetts Institute of Technology Press, 1995.

Freudenheim, L., and E. Sussman. *Building with Nature: Roots of the San Francisco Bay Region Tradition.* Santa Barbara, CA: Peregrine Smith, 1974.

Gould, Joseph E. *The Chautauqua Movement.* State University of New York, 1961.

Grattan, Virginia. *Mary Colter: Builder Upon the Red Earth.* Flagstaff, AZ: Northland Press, 1980.

Griswold, Wesley S. *A Work of Giants: Building the First Transcontinental Railroad.* New York: McGraw Hill, 1962.

Hearst, William Randolph, Jr. *The Hearsts: Father and Son.* Roberts Rinehart, Ed. 1991.

Holliday, J. S. *Rush for Riches: Gold Fever and the Making of California.* Berkeley, CA: University of California Press, 1999.

——. *The World Rushed In: The California Gold Rush Experience.* New York: Simon & Schuster, 1981.

James, Cary. *Julia Morgan.* New York: Chelsea House, 1990.

Jones, Howard M. *The Age of Energy: Varieties of American Experience 1865-1915.* New York: Viking Press, 1971.

Kastner, Victoria. *Hearst Castle: The Biography of a Country House.* New York: Harry N. Abrams, Inc. Publishers, 2000.

Keeler, Charles. *The Simple Home.* Reissued with an Introduction by Dimitri Shipounoff. Santa Barbara, CA: Peregrine Smith, 1979.

Kristeller, Paul Oskar. *The Modern System of the Arts.* Journal of the History of Ideas. Volume 12, 1951/1952.

Landes, David S. *The Unbound Prometheus: Technological Change and Industrial Development in Western Europe from 1750 to the Present.* Cambridge: Cambridge University Press, 1969.

Lears, T. J. Jackson. *No Place of Grace: Antimodernism and the Transformation of American Culture 1880-1920.* Chicago: Chicago University Press, 1983.

Lewis, Oscar. *The Big Four: The Story of Huntington, Stanford, Hopkins, and Crocker, and of the Building of the Central Pacific,* Alfred A. Knopf, ed. 1938.

Lewis, Oscar. *Here Lived the Californians.* New York: Rinehart & Co., 1957.

Longstreth, Richard. *On the Edge of the World.* Massachusetts Institute of Technology Press, 1983.

___. *Julia Morgan, Architect.* Berkeley, CA: Berkeley Architectural Heritage Association, 1977.

McLane, Lucy Neely. *A Piney Paradise.* Herald Printers, 1975.

Middleton, Robin, ed. *The Beaux-Arts and Nineteenth-Century French Architecture.* Massachusetts Institute of Technology Press, 1982.

Morgan, Keith. Charles A. *Platt: The Artist as Architect.* New York: Architectural History Foundation, 1985.

Naylor, Gillian. *The Arts and Crafts Movement.* London: Studio Vista, 1971.

Onderdonck, Francis K. *The Ferro-Concrete Style: Reinforced Concrete in Modern Architecture.* New York: Architectural Book Pub. Co., 1928.

Peterson, Charles. *"Prefabs in the California Gold Rush, 1849."* Journal of the Society of Architectural Historians, 24, no. 4 (1965): 318-324.

Priestman, Mabel. *History of the Arts and Crafts Movement in America.* Berkeley: Arts & Crafts Press, 1996.

Quacchia, Russell. Julia Morgan's Architectural Presence on the Monterey Peninsula, *"Noticias del Puerto de Monterey"*, Volume LI No. 2, Summer 2002, Monterey History and Art Association Publication.

Regnery, Dorothy. *An Enduring Heritage.* Stanford, CA: Stanford University Press, 1976.

Reiss, Susanna. *The Julia Morgan Architectural History* Project. 2 vols. Bancroft Library, University of California Regional Oral History Office, U.C., 1976.

Richey, Elinor. *"Julia Morgan—Architect with Empathy."* Eminent Women of the West. Berkeley: Howell-North Books, 1975. 237-63.

Rolle, Andrew F. *California: A History.* New York: Thomas Y. Crowell Co., 1963.

Rossi, Paolo. *Philosophy, Technology and the Arts in the Early Modern Era.* New York: Harper & Row, 1970.

Rider, David. *Great Citizen (A Biography of William H. Crocker).* San Francisco Historical Publishers,1962.

Scott, Mel. *The San Francisco Bay Area: A Metropolis in Perspective.* Berkeley, CA: University of California Press, 1959.

Scully, Vincent. *Shingle Style-Stick Style.* New Haven: Yale University Press, 1955.

Sims, Mary. *The Natural History of a Social Institution—The YWCA.* New York: The Women's Press, 1936.

Starr, Kevin. *Americans and the California Dream.* London: Oxford University Press, 1973.

Steilberg, Walter. *"Some Examples of the Work of Julia Morgan."* The Architect and Engineer of California, 55, no. 2 (November 1918):.

Stein, Roger. *John Ruskin and Aesthetic Thought in America.* Cambridge: Harvard University Press, 1967.

Taylor, F. J., and Wilson N. C. *Southern Pacific: The Story of a Fighting Railroad.* New York: McGraw-Hill, 1952.

Temko, Allan. *"The Mystery of Julia Morgan"*, review of "Julia Morgan, Architect" by Sara Holmes Boutelle, San Francisco Chronicle, July 10, 1988.

Trapp, Kenneth. *The Arts and Crafts Movement in California.* New York: Abbeville Press, 1993.

Triggs, Oscar Lovell. *Chapters in the History of the Arts and Crafts Movement.* New York: Benjamin Blom, 1971.

Wadsworth, Ginger. *Julia Morgan.* Lerner Pub., 1990.

Winter, Robert, ed. *Toward a Simpler Way of Life.* Berkeley, CA: University of California Press, 1997.

____. *"Women in Architecture."* Progressive Architecture 58 (March 1977): 42-43.

Woodbridge, Sally. *Bernard Maybeck: Visionary Architect.* New York: Abbeville Press, 1992.

____. *John Galen Howard and the University of California.* Berkeley, CA: University of California Press, 2002.

PHOTOGRAPHY CREDITS

Cover Art: Alan Dubinsky, DeSIGN Graphics (www.alandubinsky.com)

Copyright Hearst Castle/CA State Parks WRH on the phone. Figure 1.8

Photograph by Victoria Garagliano/copyright Hearst Castle/ CA State Parks. Aerial photo of Hearst Castle grounds. Figure 5.2

Julia Morgan Collection, Special Collections, California Polytechnic State University. Portrait Page, Figures 1.1, 1.2, 1.3, 2.1

Julia Morgan Collection (1959-2), Environmental Design Archives, University of California, Berkeley. Figures 1.16, 1.17, 1.18, 2.2

Courtesy of University Archives, The Bancroft Library, University of California, Berkeley. Figures 1.5, 1.6, 1.7, 1.9, 1.10, 1.11

The Architect & Engineer of California, Volume LV, Number 2, November 1918. Figure 5.4

Pat Hathaway Collection of California Views, Monterey California (URL *http://caviews.com*). Figures 1.15, 6.1, 6.2,

Note: The above lists the copyright holders for the
photograph figures shown. Photograph figures not shown are
owned by the Author. The figure numbers refer first to the
chapter location and then to photograph sequence.

INDEX

A

Academe Royal d'Architecture 206, 231
academic classicism 68, 93, 162, 164, 216. *See also* academic eclecticism
academic eclecticism 38, 68, 69, 161
Academy Platonica 231
Accademia di San Luca 232
Alexander, Harriet 126
Alta California 113, 193, 195, 197
American Institute of Architects 25, 90
ancients 210, 212, 213, 217
André, Louis Jules 78, 216, 217
Armstrong, Jane 35
Art Workers Guild 73
Arts and Crafts Movement 20, 38, 72-81, 160, 161, 165
Ashbee, Charles 73, 76
Asilomar Conference Grounds 13, 19-22, 19, 23, 38, 124-158, 189, 191, 228-229
  versus Hearst Castle 98-112
atelier 58-61

B

Bacon, Francis 212
Baja California 192, 193
balloon frame 85
Bancroft Library 227, 228, 231
Barrell, Joseph 194
Bartlett, Washington A. 199
Batchelder, Ernest A. 75, 226
Batteux, Abbe 212
Beck, J. T. 115
Bell-Clock Campanile 34
Bidwell, John 196
Big Four 89, 121, 125
Blondel, Jacques 232
Bocowald, M. 68
Bonaparte, Napoleon 215, 216
bond iron 86
Boston Ships 194
brace frame 84
Brannan, Samuel 199
Brown, A. Page 30, 77, 182
Brown, W. E. 90
Brune, Emmanuel 217
Bryant & Sturgis 194
building arts 214
Burnham, Daniel 34, 87

C

Cabrillo, Juan Rodriguez 192
Cahuenga Capitulation 198
Calafia 192
California Polytechnic State University 16, 223, 225
California Star 199

California State Park System 13
Californian 199
Carlyle, Thomas 73
Carmel 115, 128
Carmel Bay 118
Carmel-by-the-Sea 16, 229
Carmel Development Company
    229
Carrere, John Mervin 233
Carson, Kit 198
Cary, James 101
Central Pacific Company 89
Central Pacific Railroad Company
    200
Central Pacific Railway 89
Century Club of California 25, 225
charette 62
Chasussemiche, Benjamin 31, 67
Chautauqua, Lake 119
Chautauqua 118, 120
Chautauqua of the West 120
Chicago Arts and Crafts Society 74
Choisy, Auguste 93
Chronicle 87, 224
Church of the New Jerusalem 78,
    182
classical orders 217
classical rationalism 216
Club for American Women 31
Cobden-Sanderson, S. T. 73
Coffman, Taylor 17
Colbert, Jean-Baptiste 206, 208,
    213
Cole, Cornelius 89
College of Environmental Design
    Archives and Bancroft Libraries
    t Libraries 16, 223
Colter, Mary 224
Colton Hall 199
Colton, Robert 199
Columbia 194
Comstock Lode 201

concours 59, 63
concours d'emulation 63, 64
Conde, Berth 125
Conde de Monterey 192
Condit, Carl 233
Cook, James 193
Cornell University 58, 90
Cortez, Hernando 191
Coxhead, Ernest 77
Craftsman 74
Crocker Bank 89
Crocker, Charles 89, 125, 228
Crocker Dining Hall 139, 140,
    164, 174, 179, 182, 183,
    187, 220
Crocker, Ethel 128
Crocker, George 120
Crocker, William 89
Crocker, Woolworth & Co. 89

D

Da Vinci, Leonardo 231
Dana, Richard Henry, Jr.
    Two Years before the Mast 195
David Jacks County 115
De Anza, Juan Bautista 192
De Celeron, Bienville 119
De Mendoza, Antonio 192
De Monclos, Marcel 31, 61, 64, 67,
    221
De Montalva, Garaci Ordonez
    Las Sergas de Esplandian 192
De Portola, Don Gaspar 192
De Quincy, Quatremere 216
De Young, Michael 87
Del Monte Forest 113, 121, 229
Del Monte Properties Company
    121, 229
Del Monte Resort Hotel 127
Del Monte White Sand 127
Descartes, Rene 212
Devendorf, James F. 229

Di Giovanni, Bertoldo 232
Director's Cottage 174, 220
Discovery 195
Dodge Chapel 141, 142, 143, 144,
    164, 174, 178, 179, 220
Dolbeer, John 84, 96, 227
Donahue, Peter 86
Donkey Steam Engine 84, 96
Donner, George 196
Donner, Jacob 196
Duckworth, Santiago 229
Durand, N. 215
Durant, Henry F. 124

E

Ecole de Polytechnic 212, 215
Ecole des Beaux-Arts 20, 30, 31,
    32, 39, 58, 59, 69, 93, 161,
    216, 221
  history and design theory 206-
    218
Ecole des Polytechnic 215, 233
El Rio Carmelo 192
Empress of China 194
en charette 62
Enchanted Hill, The 99
Engineers Cottage 219, 220
esquisse 62
esquisses en loge 62

F

Fairmont Hotel 35, 54, 222
Farnham, Thomas
  Life and Adventures in California
    195
Federal Registry of National Land
    Marks 14
fine arts 73, 74
Five Orders 214
Fleishhacker, Mortimer 229
Forney, Lillian 161, 223

Fort Ross 196
Foye, William H. 86
Frampton, Kenneth 227
Francois-Blondel, Jacques 214
Francois-Blondel, Nicholas 209, 213
Fred Harvey Company 224
free classicism 216
free style eclecticism 212
Fremont, John C. 197
French Revolution 212, 215

G

Garnier, Tony 218
Gaudet, Julian 93, 217, 233
Geary, Blanche 126
Gold Rush 82, 100, 113, 201
Golden Spike 231
Grand Prix de Rome 60, 63, 218
grands concours 63
Great Western Paper Company 229
Guardamar 127, 128

H

Hacienda del Pozo de Verona 125
Hacienda, The 125
Hallidie, Andrew 88
Harriet Fearing residence 32
Harvard University 74
Hastings, Thomas 233
Hayward Lumber Company 227
Hearst Castle 13, 20, 160, 189
  versus Asilomar Conference
    Grounds 98-112
Hearst, George 33, 100
Hearst Mining Building 33, 221
Hearst, Phoebe 29, 32, 34, 46, 98,
    99, 100, 125, 129, 131
Hearst Social Hall 98, 105, 135,
    136, 137, 164, 166, 168,
    174, 175, 179, 180, 183,
    186, 219

Hearst, William Randolph 13, 36, 37, 47, 99, 100, 102, 103, 107, 160, 222, 223
Hennebique, Francois 227
Hidalgo, Miguel 195
Hoover, Ira Wilson 34
Hopkins, Mark 89, 125
Hotel Del Monte 117, 228
Howard, Alvinza 84
Howard, John Galen 32, 33, 34, 45, 77, 91, 98, 99, 221
Howard Street Methodist Church 116
Hubbard, Elbert 74
Huber, Walter 92
Hudson Bay Company 199
Hunt, Richard Morris 58, 233
Hunter, Abbie J. 229
Huntington, Collis 89

I

Industrial City, The 218
Industrial Revolution 72, 212, 214

J

Jacks, David 114, 115, 116, 118
Jacks Peak 115
Jackson, Andrew 196
Jordan, David Star 229
Joy, Thaddeus 35
Judah, Theodore 89

K

Kappa Alpha Theta 25, 29, 41, 99
Keeler, Charles
    Simple Home, The 78
Kohler, Charles 85
Kristeller, Oskar 232

L

La Cuesta Encantada 99
Labrouste, Henry 216, 227

Ladies Christian Association 124
Lady Washington 194
Laguna de los Ajolotes 120
Lake of the Water Dogs. See Majella, Lake
Larkin, Thomas Oliver 197
Las Manzantias Ranch 229
Las Sergas de Esplandian (De Montalva) 192
Le Duc, Viollet 217
LeBrun, Lucy 31, 64
LeBrun, Pierre 29, 31, 34, 64, 67
Ledyard, John 193
Lees, Jacob P. 199
Leland Stanford Junior Museum 87, 231
Lelia Byrd 194
Lemmonier, Henry 217
Lemmonier, M. 69
LeRoy, Julian D. 232
Lethaby, William R. 73
Life and Adventures in California (Farnham) 195
Lincoln, Abraham 200
Literary Academe Francaise 231
Lodge Buildings 164, 180, 182
Louis XIII 231
Louis XIV 206
Louis XVIII 216
Louvre 213

M

Mackintosh, Charles Rennie 73
Majella Depot 127
Majella, Lake 118, 120
Margaret Carnegie Library 34, 52, 53, 221
Marshall, James W. 198
Massachusetts Institute of Technology (MIT) 58
massier 60
Maybeck, Bernard 16, 30, 31, 32,

44, 59, 64, 67, 68, 77, 78,
173, 217, 221, 223
McKim, Mead & White 35, 78
McMurray, Lynn Forney 223
mechanical arts 212, 224
Mechanics Lien Law 90
Merchant Exchange Building 221
Merrill Hall 155, 156, 157, 158,
174, 179, 183, 220
Merrill, Mary 128
Merritt, Lake 225
Methodist Retreat Association 115
Mexican War 114, 195, 198
Miller, Lewis 119
Mills College 16, 34, 51, 52, 53,
91, 124, 221, 230
Mining and Greek Theater projects
34, 91, 130
Mizner, Addison 233
Monroe Doctrine, The 196
Monterey City 113, 114, 117
Monterey Jack cheese 115
Monterey-Salinas Valley Railroad
117
Morgan, Avery 23, 28
Morgan, Charles 26, 27, 200
Morgan, Eliza 23, 27, 29, 221
Morgan, Emma 23, 28, 29
Morgan, Gardiner 23
Morgan, Julia 13, 19-22, 58-59
architectural career 91, 98-112,
159-161
architectural training 58-69
Asilomar buildings 159-187
site plan 221
design approach 37-39, 92, 161-
165
education 28-31
family 23, 26-28
Hearst Castle versus Asilomar
Conference Grounds 98-112
organizations 25

relationship with August Perret
92-94
time line 221-222
Morgan, Parmelee 23
Morris, Samuel E. 121
Morris, William 73, 75
Morse, John F. 226
Morse, Samuel 88
Morse, Samuel F. B. 228
Muir, John 77
Mullgardt, Louis 77
Murdoch, Iris 165

N

Napoleon LeBrun & Sons 29
National Bank of San Francisco 89
Nesbit, Evelyn 35
New Helvetia 196
New York Commodity Exchange 27
New York Metropolitan Life
Insurance 29
North, Flora 223
North, Morgan 223
Norton, Charles Eliot 74

O

Oakland High School 28, 221
Order of Our Lady of Mount
Carmel 192

P

Pacific Grove 13, 19, 20, 108, 113,
114, 116, 117, 118, 120,
122, 123, 126, 127, 129,
189, 202, 229
Pacific Grove Retreat Association
117
Pacific Improvement Company
117, 118, 121, 126, 228
Pacific Lighting Company 88
Pacific Railroad Bill 200

Pacific Railway Act of 1862 89
Pacific Region National Board 124
Pacific Stone Company 87
Panama-Pacific International
    Exposition 33
Pattie, James 196
Pebble Beach 99, 113, 121
Peixotto, Jessica 28, 29, 31, 59
Perault, Claude 213
Perret, August 93, 94, 227
Pico, Andres 198
Piedmont Hills 76
Pirate's Den 174
Platt, Charles 174
Polk, Willis 77
Portsmouth Square 198, 199
Powers, Frank 229
Presidio San Francisco de Assisi 192
Promontory Point 200, 231
Pugin, A. W. N. 38, 73, 159

R

Rancho Aquajito 115
Rancho El Pescadero 115, 116
Rancho Punta de Pinos 115, 116
Rancho San Antonio 225
Ransome, Ernest 87, 92
Rape of Monterey, The 114
Registry of National Landmarks 173
Richards, Grace Fisher 99
Richardson, Henry H. 216
Richardson, W. A. 198
Richelieu 231
Rider, David W. 226
Riess, Susanna 227, 228, 230
Robert F. Kennedy Library 16, 223
Roberts, Marshall O. 124
Rocky Mountains 197
Ross, W. S. 115
Royal Academy of Architecture
    207, 208, 210, 213, 215,
    216, 232

Royal Academy of Science 233
Roycroft Shops 74
Ruskin, John 73, 74

S

Sacramento Valley 196
Salisbury, Helen 129
San Francisco Bay Region 19, 20,
    39, 72-81, 117
    construction methods 84-88
San Francisco Call 35, 87
San Francisco Society of Architects
    90
San Francisco Women's Athletic
    Club 25
San Simeon 13, 21, 99, 101, 102,
    104, 105, 107, 108, 109,
    160, 222, 230
Santa Cruz County 124
Santa Fe Railroad Company 224
Santa Lucia Mountains 101
School of Architecture 90
School of Civil Engineering 90
Schooley, Ella 129
Schweinfurth, Albert 77, 78
Scott, Mackay Hugh Bailey 73
Scripps Lodge 145, 146, 182, 220
Semple, Robert 199
Shaler, William 194
Shasta Iron Works 27
Shaws, William 194
Shepard, Adam D. 126
Simple Home, The (Keeler) 78
Smeaton, John 90
Smith, Jedediah 196
Some Examples of the Work of Julia
    Morgan (Steilberg) 37
Soule, Frank 30
Southern Pacific Company 89
Southern Pacific Railroad 116
St. John's Presbyterian Church 79,
    183

Stanford, Leland 16, 87, 89, 125, 231
Stanford Museum 92
Stanford University 16, 76, 87, 90, 129, 228, 229
State Constitutional Convention 199
Steilberg, Walter 37, 92, 102, 103
Some Examples of the Work of Julia Morgan 106, 183, 227, 228
Stewardson, John 233
Stickley, Gustav 74
Strait of Anian 192
Strickland, William 86
strict classicism 212, 213, 214
Structural Analysis of the Steel Frame of the Mills Building in San Francisco 30
Stuck-up Inn 174, 181, 182, 220
style adaptation 215
Sullivan, Louis 217
Sunday School Association 119
Sunday School Movement 119
Sunset Magazine 120
Sutter, Johann Augustus 196
Sutter, John A. 198

T

Taylor, Augustine 85
Taylor, Harriet 126
Tchadakoin 119
Temko, Allan 189, 224
Territory of Utah 231
Thaw, Harry K. 35
Thomas, John Hudson 77
Thompson, Waddy 197
Thornton, Lucy 29
Treaty of Guadalupe Hidalgo 198, 199
Triggs, Oscar Lovel 74
Two Years before the Mast (Dana) 195
Tyler, John 197

U

Union Iron Works Company 86
Union Pacific 89, 231
Unitarian Church of the New Jerusalem 182
University of California 15, 25, 28, 30, 31, 32, 38, 58, 79, 90, 98, 99, 163, 221, 223
University of Chicago 74

V

Vancouver, George 195
Vasari, Giorgio 232
Vaudremer, August 217
Vincent, John Heyle 119
Vitruvius, Marcus 159, 213, 232
Vizcaino, Sebastian 191, 192
Voysey, C. F. A. 73

W

Wadsworth, Ginger 225
Walker, Joseph 196
Webb, Philip 73
West Point 90
Western platform frame 85, 97
Western Union Company 88
Wheeler, Benjamin Ide 129
Wheeler, Ide (Mrs. Benjamin Wheeler) 128
White, Stanford 35
Wilkes, Charles 197
Wimmer, Elizabeth 231
Wimmer Nugget 231
Wimmer, Peter 198
Women's Athletic Club of San Francisco 25, 225
Wood Dove Lake. *See* Majella, Lake
Woodbridge, Sally 159
Worcester, Joseph 76, 77, 78, 182
Wotton, Sir Henry 159

Y

Yerba Buena 198
Yosemite Valley 77
Young Ladies Christian Association
      124
Young Women's Christian
      Association (YWCA) 13, 20,
      36, 98, 99, 100, 107, 108,
      120, 124, 125, 128, 131,
      161, 175, 180, 189, 202,
      222, 224

About the Author

Russell Quacchia is a native of San Francisco and a graduate of the University of California, School of Architecture at Berkeley. He practiced architecture in San Francisco and was a partner in the firm of John Funk & Associates for many years. Until recently he has been an architectural project manager at Stanford University and is now an independent architectural consultant. He resides in Los Altos and in Carmel-by-the-Sea.